PROTECT

A YOUTH WORKER'S GUIDE
TO NAVIGATING RISK

Protect: A Youth Worker's Guide to Navigating Risk

Copyright © 2019 by Jody Dean. All rights reserved.
Published by youthministry360, in the United States of America.

ISBN 10: 1935832794
ISBN 13: 9781935832799

No part of this publication may be reproduced, stored in a retrieval system, or transmitted in any form or by any means electronic or mechanical, including photocopy, audio recording, digital scanning, or any information storage and retrieval system now known or to be invented, without prior permission in writing from the publisher.

Any reference within this piece to Internet addresses of websites not under the administration of youthministry360 is not to be taken as an endorsement of these websites by youthministry360; neither does youthministry360 vouch for their content.

Unless otherwise noted, Scripture quotations are from the ESV® Bible (The Holy Bible, English Standard Version®), copyright © 2001 by Crossway, a publishing ministry of Good News Publishers. Used by permission. All rights reserved.

Executive Editor
Andy Blanks

Art Director
Laurel-Dawn Latshaw

Copy Editor
Paige Townley

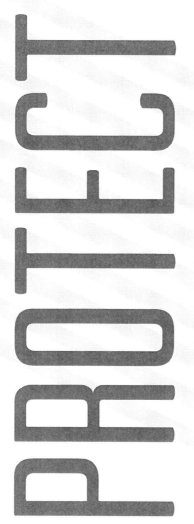

PROTECT

A YOUTH WORKER'S GUIDE TO NAVIGATING RISK

BY DR. JODY DEAN WITH DR. ALLEN JACKSON

FOREWORD BY GREG LOVE

Published by: YM360

TABLE OF CONTENTS

Foreword — 8

Introduction — 12

PART 1: SHEPHERDING THROUGH CHARACTER
Chapter 1: The Critical Component of Character by Dr. Allen Jackson — 18
Chapter 2: Vetting the Volunteers by Dr. Jody Dean — 22
Chapter 3: Making Money Matter by Dr. Jody Dean — 27

PART 2: SHEPHERDING THE PEOPLE
Chapter 4: Counseling Considerations by Dr. Allen Jackson — 34
Chapter 5: Practicing Protective Procedures by Dr. Jody Dean — 39
Chapter 6: Owning Online Obnoxiousness by Dr. Jody Dean — 44
Chapter 7: Bursting the Bullying Balloon by Dr. Jody Dean — 48

PART 3: THE SHEPHERD AS AN OVERSEER
Chapter 8: Mastering Mandatory Reporting by Dr. Allen Jackson — 54
Chapter 9: Supervision, Surveillance, and Security by Dr. Jody Dean — 58
Chapter 10: Preparing Proper Policy by Dr. Jody Dean — 62
Chapter 11: Keeping Up with the Kids by Dr. Jody Dean — 66
Chapter 12: Unpacking the Unexpected by Dr. Jody Dean — 70

PART 4: SHEPHERDING THE ENVIRONMENT AND CULTURE
Chapter 13: Facing Faulty Facilities by Dr. Jody Dean — 76
Chapter 14: Tripping Up on Trips by Dr. Jody Dean — 80
Chapter 15: Negating Negligence by Dr. Jody Dean — 84
Chapter 16: Considering Contemporary Issues by Dr. Allen Jackson — 88

Conclusion — 92

About the Authors — 97

FOREWORD

Writing the foreword for this book is an honor and a privilege because I hold the authors in the highest regard and I believe the subject matter to be of the utmost importance.

As I write this, I have been practicing law for nearly 30 years, primarily in the realm of child sexual abuse litigation, prevention, and risk management. I am a partner in the law firm Love & Norris, and a co-founder and Director of MinistrySafe and Abuse Prevention Systems. In these capacities, I serve thousands of organizations: churches of all denominations, para-church organizations, camps, schools, youth sports organizations, daycares, non-profits, and other child-serving entities. I am honored to work in this realm in a multitude of contexts, but my heart beats fast for the Church – particularly youth ministry.

In addition to practicing law since 1990, I am beginning my 23rd year of student ministry at Christ Chapel Bible Church in Fort Worth, TX. For the last several years, I have served as the speaker for our Student Ministry ski trips. At a recent trip to Winter Park, CO, my goal was to address the challenges and obstacles that teenagers face related to spiritual growth.

My challenge was two-fold:
    1. *What* information do teens need to hear; and
    2. *How* to deliver information in a manner that students were reached, without losing the seriousness of the message.

WHAT: THE MESSAGE
The focus of my messages was relatively straightforward: identifying and overcoming the barriers to spiritual growth faced by teenagers today. The message was important, but some teenagers are suspicious of authority and ready to ignore or reject instruction that requires change or inconvenience. My desire was not to burden them with another spiritual to-do list, but to show how Christ created the model and plan for abundant life.

HOW: THE DELIVERY
This part is tricky. As you no doubt know, unpacking spiritual truth in a manner that teenagers will understand, appreciate, appropriate, and apply takes a great deal of insight and creativity. The effectiveness of this endeavor has a great deal to do with the identity of the person communicating. Fortunately, I serve a population of teenagers who trust me as a "coach," not a "referee."

After my experience at our ski retreat, I very much appreciate the value of *Protect*. Drs. Jody Dean and Allen Jackson faced the same challenge: What information do youth workers need to hear; and how to deliver information in a manner that youth workers are reached, without losing the seriousness of the message.

WHAT: THE MESSAGE
The focus of *Protect* is relatively straightforward: what risks are inherent in youth ministry that must be understood and addressed to protect students and those who serve them? The subject matter is essential. And yet, if we're honest, many youth ministry leaders (like many teenagers) are ready to ignore or reject instruction that requires change or inconvenience. If this describes you, you have to be willing to work to overcome this tendency; the subject matter is that important.

HOW: THE DELIVERY
Clearly, Dean and Jackson have worked to avoid writing anything resembling a treatise on the law, also avoiding the typical reliance on guilt, threats, and fear to introduce relevant information and urge change. I believe you will find that *Protect* strikes the right balance: clear, but not intimidating; informative, but not over-the-top; serious, but not threatening. *Protect* is encouraging, in that most youth pastors can connect with one or two of the situations unpacked, and readers will quickly intuit that the writers know youth ministry and can save them a few unnecessary trips through the ditch.

Much of the "how" of this book is related to the "who." In youth ministry, there is a tendency among some youth ministry leaders to view older leaders as outdated and out of touch with the challenges unique to younger generations. Often they are right. At the same time, many youth ministry leaders rely heavily on the advice and suggestions of their peers, attending conferences or network gatherings where the speakers are just a few years older than they are. Unfortunately, many of these venues do not provide the information and understanding necessary to properly navigate the challenges facing youth ministry leaders today, especially those challenges related to risk management and child protection.

That's why the "who" of this book is so important. Jody Dean is a unique blend of youth ministry veteran and administrative consultant. He has taken on the responsibility of teaching and researching risk management at New Orleans Baptist Seminary, partnering with relevant voices including MinistrySafe.

Allen Jackson has served in youth ministry for almost 40 years. Through his work over the years at NOBTS, the Youth Ministry Institute, Youth Specialties, and elsewhere, thousands upon thousands of youth pastors in the United States have been coached by Dr. Jackson, and continue to count him as a friend, mentor, and role model.

PROTECT: THE BEGINNING OF THE ADVENTURE
As mentioned above, *Protect* communicates information unique to youth ministry lead-

ers in such a way that youth leaders will connect, understand, appreciate, appropriate, and apply the information. *Protect* starts the conversation. In many respects, there is more work to do. To this end, *Protect* identifies and discusses the necessary topics, and references appropriate tools and resources useful in ministry contexts.

One such tool is MinistrySafe, which provides state-of-the-art tools and online trainings designed to help prevent child sexual abuse in ministry contexts. MinistrySafe was created by attorneys who prosecute sexual abuse cases, and who routinely provide legal counsel related to child sexual abuse. To learn more, visit MinistrySafe.com.

Another critical resource is MinistrySafe Institute, providing 17+ hours of seminary level, cutting-edge online training meant to equip ministry leaders with an understanding of the issues surrounding child sexual abuse, and how best to navigate through them. Trainees who complete all course modules receive MinistrySafe Institute Certification, demonstrating a commitment to the highest standards of preventative protocols and training available to ministry leaders today. To learn more, visit MinistrySafeInstitute.com.

Drs. Jody Dean and Allen Jackson have created an excellent on-ramp and roadmap for youth ministers to begin the adventure regarding the protection of youth, staff, and the ministry. I applaud this vital effort to raise the barriers of protection in youth ministry occurring in American churches today.

Greg Love
Co-Founder/Director
MinistrySafe

INTRODUCTION

Youth ministry has matured since the days of chubby bunny and the egg-and-armpit relay. We have a tremendous opportunity to challenge an information-rich generation to consider the life-changing claims of Christ. A couple of other things have changed as well. First, the world has, in some ways, become more dangerous. Roads are more crowded, communities are less cohesive, and online communication has made students more connected–and accessible–than ever before. Second, parents have a reasonable yet heightened expectation that youth ministry, school, athletic teams, and other places inhabited by students would be safe–safe from dangerous conditions and safe from dangerous persons. *Protect* attempts to come alongside those who guide youth ministry in churches and parachurch organizations to engage in the practice of risk management.

My world was rocked in February 2015 when the accusations of sexual impropriety on the part of the youth minister at our church came to light. The accusations turned out to be true and likely the tip of the iceberg. I met with him, and he denied that anything occurred other than poor judgment with the wording of some text messages. As is often the case with predators, he was very convincing. It turns out he molested a student in the youth ministry through systematic grooming.

Our pastor modeled the right legal and ethical response to the criminal actions of a staff member, but by then it was too late to protect the young person involved. It was particularly offensive to me because I have taught this subject for years in my seminary classroom and conferences and workshops around the country. I have hosted my friend Greg Love and others who heroically kept the issue of child protection in front of youth ministers and churches. Yet it happened in my church.

I am reminded of the Surgeon General's warnings on cigarette packages. They have been on the edge or bottom of every pack that has been sold in America for the past four decades. Yet, they have become white noise, so that while smoking is understood as harmful to one's health, the dialogue about the danger has simply died down.

This book is an attempt to reignite the discussion on risk management in youth ministry. Protection of our students is the most urgent aspect of the conversation, both from predators and other harmful conditions in ministry. But protection for the ministry is also necessary: protection from harmful or useless practices, from damage to our witness, and for ministers and volunteers in an increasingly litigious culture.

Dr. Dean and I decided to write this book because it hasn't been done in a while. We are not lawyers, but we have consulted lawyers. We are not insurance people, but we have consulted insurance people. We are parents, ministers, and men who care deeply for students, the volunteers who work with them, and the churches that facilitate this crazy thing called youth ministry. We hope that we inspire confidence that youth ministry really can be both fun and safe. Finally, we want to honor King Jesus with our words, our practices, and our counsel.

A WORD ABOUT THOSE WHO HELPED US FRAME THE DISCUSSION

We were inspired and encouraged to write this book by many different people. Youth workers from around the country helped guide our discussions for a resource that would help them start a conversation with leaders and parents in their churches about the urgency to protect the people that gather on church campuses each week. Parents have guided our thoughts as we have sat with many crying over their child being robbed of their innocence by an adult who took advantage of their trust and harmed their child in some way. And students have stopped by the office, chatted with us at an event, or sent us an email that revealed the need for a resource that provided a collective starting point for conversation and resources to protect in one or more of the areas mentioned in this book.

A WORD ABOUT WHAT WE ARE NOT WRITING ABOUT

We chose not to be as detailed in the content as we might have been, but to instead provide an overview for each area as a point of discussion and information that would cause you to pray, discern, research, and choose how to protect your students, yourself, your ministry, and your church. We chose to leave the legal details to the lawyers. We chose to let the accountants explain the financial guidelines beyond common sense basics. We chose to let MinistrySafe help you understand volunteer screening after we made the case that you need to use applications and screening for volunteers and staff in the church.

We chose to not address all the hot topics of culture but tried instead to provide a conversation on the shifting culture and the need for us to consider the new norm as we chart new paths. You can read the headlines like we have relating to the issues involving ministry. Here are just a few that were in the news as we were beginning to write this book:

- In Washington, a youth pastor sent sexually explicit emails to a girl in the youth group. He was sentenced to 30 years in prison.
- A different type of risk happened in Florida, where a 15-passenger van transporting a church youth group rolled killing one person.
- In Oregon, another tragedy occurred during a retreat when a 15-year-old boy and an adult camp counselor fell into a pool at the base of a waterfall during a youth retreat involving multiple churches. Both drowned. The family of the boy sued the camp organizer and churches for $13 million.[1]

Headlines such as these abound. These examples are all tragic, and we pray they never occur at your church or while you are doing ministry. Stories like these helped motivate us to write this book.

YOUTH MINISTRY IS A *STAFF* POSITION

A shepherd's staff, that is. I read an article that discussed the staff a shepherd uses to do his job of tending the wooly ones.[2] The author mentioned three ways the staff is essential. The connection with care for the students with whom we minister and the youth ministry we lead was overwhelming to me.

First, the staff is used to gather newly-born lambs and make sure they are placed with their mother. In a large flock, the mother and child can become separated, and if the shepherd leaves a scent on the lamb, the ewe will reject her lamb. In the same way, we protect our students by making sure they are with those adult volunteers who will care for them in all the right ways.

Secondly, the staff is used to draw sheep to the shepherd for inspection. The famous crook in the staff is used to make sure that the sheep are healthy and clear of environmental danger. Risk management means that we are "inspecting" students, alert to changes in their demeanor that might signal a problem, and always aware of surroundings and potential problems (i.e., volunteers, workers, peers, strangers, predators, etc.). A shepherd knows what to look for and is always examining the surroundings of his flock and those within the flock.

Finally, the staff is used to direct the sheep to places they need to go and away from places they don't need to go. The shepherd leads the flock so they do not stray or go in a different direction. Policies, protective measures, and procedures sometimes protect students from themselves. We know that teenagers are prone to wander toward risky behavior, like the sheep who tend to wander off, thinking the pasture is greener somewhere else. Risk management practices sometimes are the gentle prod that the shepherd gives to distracted or rebellious sheep. The prodding may be annoying and uncomfortable to the sheep, but it keeps them moving in the direction they need to go.

Before I leave the metaphor, I would also point out that first-century shepherds would frequently sleep while lying down across the opening to the sheepfold (pen) to make sure anything that would threaten the flock would have to come through him first. That is why Jesus, speaking of Himself said, "The Good Shepherd lays down his life for his sheep." Without being overly dramatic, the hard work of putting into place practices that keep students and ministries as safe as possible is like a youth minister, pastor, or volunteer saying, "if you are going to get to my students, you have to come through me."

A final word of introduction. Throughout the book, we use the term "risk management" because we understand youth ministry involves the possibility of negative things happening. Kids have accidents, unforeseen and sometimes tragic situations occur, and sometimes harm comes the way of a student despite the most diligent practices. That is why the term is risk management and not risk elimination. If youth ministry were utterly free of any risk, it would not only be amazingly dull, it would also be completely static. Our job is to seek to make disciples among teenagers and adults while keeping potential risk to a minimum.

- Dr. Allen Jackson

PART 1

SHEPHERDING THROUGH CHARACTER

In this section, we look at how important it is that youth pastors have a good reputation, earned through a life of integrity. It follows logically that volunteers would be expected to have a good reputation as well, and the expectation of parents (and of insurance companies) is that we will conduct background checks on any person who works with a minor in any capacity. Next, we talk about keeping up with the kids–check in, check out, drop off procedures, etc. Finally, we speak to the utilization of church resources in a way that is competent and inspires confidence in parents and church members who invest in youth ministry, either through offerings or registration.

CHAPTER ONE: THE CRITICAL COMPONENT OF CHARACTER

BY DR. ALLEN JACKSON

I am glad that this chapter opens up our discussion. You might be a full-time youth pastor. You might be a part-time student minister. You might be a volunteer, a parent, a student, or a casual observer of youth ministry. But you wouldn't be reading this book if you didn't have concerns about making sure that students were protected in your student ministry. You already have an intuitive sense that things are not right in our world and that to the best of our ability, we should keep students from harm. Guess what? It starts with us.

Character matters. I am writing this after voters in the United States shocked the American media and the world by electing Donald Trump as our forty-fifth president. Throughout the campaign, character concerns about both candidates (Trump and Hillary Clinton) were cycled and recycled in the news. In an op-ed piece in the Washington Post, entitled, "The GOP is learning the hard way that character matters," conservative columnist Michael Gerson tried to get his arms around the discussion (and threw in a little C.S. Lewis' *Mere Christianity* along the way):

> Since Thomas Jefferson's concubine, Warren Harding's love nest and Bill Clinton's innovative intern program, Americans have debated the role of character in leadership. But the concept of character has often been defined too narrowly. Sexual ethics — involving a range of behaviors from doomed longing to cruel exploitation — is a part of it, but not the most significant part. "The sins of the flesh are bad," wrote C.S. Lewis, "but they are the least bad of all sins. All the worst pleasures are purely spiritual: the pleasure of putting other people in the wrong, of bossing and patronizing and spoiling sport, and back-biting; the pleasures of power, of hatred."[3]

I am afraid the many of the issues we talk about in this book are mentioned or implied in Gerson's article. And sometimes, we define the concept of character too narrowly for those of us who are privileged to work with teenagers and their parents. Character is the framework of belief we bring to our position as youth worker. It is our perception of who we are in relationship to God, to students, to families, our pastor, and our community. Its importance cannot be overstated.

A minister or volunteer who keeps their character above reproach has put in place the best defense against any accusation that comes their way. Let me illustrate. If someone falsely accuses me of misconduct, either formally or in an impromptu gossip session, one response by the hearer could be "Wait a minute buddy. I know Allen and what you say is inconsistent with all I know him to be." On the other hand, someone might say, "Well, I can see that. Allen forwarded a questionable email just the other day and last week, he told me a vulgar joke. I hope it isn't true, but it wouldn't shock me." Now, which response do I want when a false accusation is brought forward?

Among many biblical instructions regarding character, Paul wrote to Timothy regarding the qualities of a minister (and by implication, volunteer):

> "[1] The saying is trustworthy: If anyone aspires to the office of overseer, he desires a noble task. [2] Therefore an overseer must be above reproach, the husband of one wife, sober-minded, self-controlled, respectable, hospitable, able to teach, [3] not a drunkard, not violent but gentle, not quarrelsome, not a lover of money. [4] He must manage his own household well, with all dignity keeping his children submissive, [5] for if someone does not know how to manage his own household, how will he care for God's church? [6] He must not be a recent convert, or he may become puffed up with conceit and fall into the condemnation of the devil. [7] Moreover, he must be well thought of by outsiders, so that he may not fall into disgrace, into a snare of the devil. [8] Deacons likewise must be dignified, not double-tongued, not addicted to much wine, not greedy for dishonest gain. [9] They must hold the mystery of the faith with a clear conscience. [10] And let them also be tested first; then let them serve as deacons if they prove themselves blameless."
> - 1 Timothy 3:1–10

Without getting sidetracked by all the tangents this passage has taken the church on, it should be noted that Paul mentions character more than he does ability or skill. He challenges Timothy to identify and deploy leaders who are temperate, prudent, respectable, gentle, peaceable, not greedy or materialistic, dignified, and not proud. Paul also wants the leaders in the church to have good reputations in the church, but also the community. Character matters.

The possibility of an accusation is not the only motivation for establishing a good reputation. First of all, we answer to God. The Psalmist said, "Let the words of my mouth and the meditation of my heart be acceptable in your sight, O LORD, my rock and my redeemer" (Psalm 19:14). I hope that I am motivated by the gratitude I feel because Jesus has redeemed me, and I do not want to disregard that grace gift. Additionally, the example of a life lived with integrity is a great living lesson for students. If we as youth workers model obedience and excellence, some students will observe and imitate. (A caution here: we cannot act one way in front of students to be a good example and another way when we are alone or with other adults. Students can see through hypocrisy like nobody else can.)

One system of checks and balances when discussing character is accountability. Accountability is a popular buzzword, yet it is a critical component that requires devoted and constant attention in the life of all disciples, but especially in this context. As I said in the last paragraph, each of us should understand that we are accountable to God as Christians for our thoughts, our actions, and our example. Also, Christians are accountable to the local body of believers that enlisted them to serve. In 2 Samuel, David finally yielded to accountability when Nathan confronted him with his sin. As a result, reconciliation with God and man could begin, though the consequences of David's choices remained.

Another level of accountable relationship is to the church as a body of believers. We youth ministers are given what is referred to as "fiduciary trust," meaning that we are to care for something or someone entrusted to us in a way that is in their best interest. Parents, other staff, church leaders all expect us to set up systems, activities, programs, and relationships that are in the best interest of teenagers.

The congregation should provide oversight to the work and by extension, the character of the leaders.

Each person is accountable to their family for the life they lead in private as well as public. The broader community and even society as a whole bring a level of accountability for the local church and its leaders. "Biblically we are to be accountable to God, to the Christian community, and, in some ways, to civic government and the community in which we minister. The Lord has created us with the need to be accountable to him and others. When we aren't, we're not only disobedient to God's Word, we're likely to get ourselves into trouble, even scandal."[4] In other words, we represent our church in the way we conduct ourselves.

My friend, Troy Temple, identified in his doctoral dissertation character qualities related to effective youth ministry.[5] Among the qualities that facilitate fiduciary trust were:

      1. Be above reproach in conduct with youth and adults.
      2. Be authentic so what they say matches what they do.
      3. Have a humility grounded in obedience to God.
      4. Seek to be led by the Spirit.
      5. Be a supporter of the senior or lead pastor in word and attitude.
      6. Contribute to church staff unity.
      7. Demonstrate integrity in finances both personal and ministerial.
      8. Have a high regard for the truth.
      9. Demonstrate personal discipline in their personal life: body, mind, and time management.

10. Be committed to moral purity.
11. Be emotionally stable with very few mood swings.

Character matters in our appearances. The ability to "be above reproach" (#1) is an external evaluation, and the only data that people can gather is the observation that one conducts relationships with integrity. To follow through with verbal commitments (#2, #8) is to establish a baseline for trust. To support church leadership and foster unity (#5, #6) is to affirm and respect authority.

To demonstrate integrity in finances (#7) and to demonstrate personal discipline in life management (#9) is to exemplify the biblical principle of faithfulness in the small things = ability to handle large things (Matthew 25:23). Increasingly, credit scores, debt portfolio, and financial health are legitimate issues when a youth pastor is called to a local church. Personal discipline in personal fitness and time management is rightly connected to discipline in protecting students.

Character shows through work ethic, through reaction under stress, through attention to detail, through punctuality. Whether we like it or understand it, the perception of a youth pastor's or youth volunteer's ability to manage the safety and well-being of students in our care.

Character is "inside out" rather than "outside in." The desire to be a person of integrity should not be based on fear of being caught, accused, or sued. Instead, our prayer is that we cultivate a lifestyle such that our desire matches with David's. We should want God to refine our heart.

Thomas Paine once said, "Reputation is what men and women think of us. Character is what God and the angels know of us."[6] I would affirm Paine, who was known for his common sense (pun intended), but I would add that reputation (what men and women think of us) is essential as it inspires confidence and deflects accusations. However, character (what God knows of us) is the essence of protecting our life, ministry, family, and future.

CHAPTER TWO: VETTING THE VOLUNTEERS

BY DR. JODY DEAN

Sunday morning: In the craziness between worship, age-graded ministry, and small groups, I encountered a couple (who had been attending our church) inquiring about how they might serve within our ministry. I walked up to one of our greeters freely sharing about all our ministries and age-graded options with children and students. I waited for a break and then engaged this couple in a conversation.

I began our conversation with some small talk, then dug a little deeper. I asked about their faith, and what it was about serving in our student ministry they felt called to. I discovered they were relatively new to our area and had only visited our church a few times. As you might imagine, I began to slow the process down a bit.

You may ask why, in a ministry that needed volunteers, why would I soft peddle the process? Great question. In the ensuing weeks, as we continued the conversation, a background check came back and revealed some concerns for these people serving with minors. If I had fast-tracked their desire to serve because we needed adult volunteers, I might have very well put a teenager at risk. It was yet another example of why good risk management policies help provide guardrails for our ministry efforts.

A vetting process is crucial in our changing culture to be able to protect those under our care. I not only recommend vetting volunteers for their moral behavior but also their salvation and ongoing discipleship journey. We train our first impressions volunteers and greeters to be friendly to new people as well as members. However, we also have to be aware that we can share too much information too quickly with guests.

Much of the attention in the discussion of risk management and legal issues is rightly directed toward worker-screening and integrity of any person who works with minors in the church. Families who visit your church are beginning to ask about policies and procedures in place to keep toxic adults away from students. Volunteer screening is a huge deal. The safeguarding of your ministry through the selection of adults within your church is going to be the focus of our discussion.

Many components for safety and security should be a high priority for your ministry, but standards should first be in place for sound doctrine, spiritual maturity, and the discipleship of the potential volunteer. Since a volunteer that serves as a host home, chaperone, or small group leader could be a key person for guiding a teenager in their salvation or through a crisis moment in their life, the following suggestions should be considered.

In vetting a potential volunteer, you should first seek to know their salvation experience and personal testimony. The spiritual climate of their family of origin could be indicators to how they might relate to teenagers. It's possible this will need to be addressed. Their church membership and key personal doctrine should be based on your church's stated beliefs. A potential volunteer should be willing to teach and lead in compliance with the guiding documents of your church. For instance, in my denomination, a volunteer that does not believe the Bible is the inspired, infallible, and inherent Word of God should not be considered in a volunteer teaching role in our church. You may have similar denominational distinctives you would hold your volunteers accountable to. The point is that vetting volunteers for spiritual and doctrinal issues is first and foremost.

Why is this true? Consider the adult chaperone on a youth trip. What if he or she is not advancing in their walk with Christ? He or she may not be the best person for the trip. So many questions about life and Christianity can be raised, and you want someone who is already experiencing Christ in their life. The ability to disciple another person should be a paramount consideration when the goal of youth ministry should be to reach and make disciples. I consider personal faith and a walk with God just as important as the screening and background check process. In ministry, I believe we have to be willing to disqualify staff or volunteers for all these concerns.

In the last few years, the public awareness of seemingly unsuspecting adults engaging in inappropriate and sinful behavior has surfaced in news feeds, social media, and the nightly newsreels. Jesus revealed in His teaching the need to protect the minors under our watch. The illustration for the disciples of the hierarchy of the kingdom in heaven is revealing for us as we discern the importance of vetting the volunteers:

> "[3] and said, "Truly, I say to you, unless you turn and become like children, you will never enter the kingdom of heaven. [4] Whoever humbles himself like this child is the greatest in the kingdom of heaven. [5] "Whoever receives one such child in my name receives me, [6] but whoever causes one of these little ones who believe in me to sin, it would be better for him to have a great millstone fastened around his neck and to be drowned in the depth of the sea." (Matthew 18:3–6)

While many takeaways can be gleaned from this passage, one can discern that the adults ministering to minors in the church should take their actions and words seriously, understanding the great responsibility they have been given.

There seems to be a tendency within some organizations to have stricter risk management procedures for children than there are for teenagers. As you create a system to screen your volunteers, the process must be followed by everyone and be applied to all people in the church who desire to serve in ministry with minors . . . any minors. The safeguards for your church should not be reduced for any ministry or anyone.

Youth ministry deals with adolescents (legally considered minors) who have the same protections as a child when it comes to an adult's illegal conduct toward them. America created the concept of an adolescent in the twentieth century with the creation of child labor laws, public high school, and many other changes in the social order which resulted in an extended childhood before entering into adulthood. We see this through the observance of the military draft, the right to vote, and age restrictions on alcohol. The legal line for adulthood is firm, and the youth ministry in your church needs to safeguard teenagers from adults who could cause harm due to physical, verbal, or emotional abuse.

As you begin to craft processes that help you manage risk, you may want to keep in mind the following considerations:

FOLLOW THE TWO-PERSON RULE
The two-person rule says that no teenager or child will at any time be in the care of a single adult; there should always be more than one adult with a child or teenager. This is a reasonably wide-spread rule and one that is easy to begin implementing in your ministry. (Also, I would add that it's ideal that the two people in charge of supervising an individual youth shouldn't be spouses. Under a principle called spousal privilege, a married couple does not have to testify against the other in court. This may need to be considered when making allowances for married couples to be the only adults in charge of a single student.)

Youth ministry utilizes parents and other adults as volunteers to chaperone, mentor, teach, and often open their homes for various events. The two-person rule should extend to the various ways adults interact with teenagers for the protection of the adult and the minor. When a parent offers to drop off another student on their way home or is left alone with one student waiting for parents to pick-up, their child should still have two adults to protect them. Another student is still a minor and could be less than accurate in their retelling of the events that transpire with their peer.

CONSIDER RECORDED VIDEO SURVEILLANCE
Surveillance systems have reduced in price significantly over the past few years. They are an excellent tool in eliminating any doubt over what occurred in the youth room or class. My suggestion would include an option with audio, not just video. School systems have embraced this technology for protecting students and adults alike (think about the cameras installed on buses). I would strongly encourage you to consider it on any church-owned vehicles as well.

THINK TWICE ABOUT MINORS SUPERVISING MINORS

A church should consider the age of workers regarding a minor supervising another minor. A teenager hanging out at your church with a parent creates potential issues and liability. You can imagine the heartache and the headache of a child or another teenager being injured under the supervision of a teenager. Many churches are surprised to find out that their insurance doesn't cover liability when the person supervising isn't an adult.

The desire to make disciples creates a unique issue with volunteers. The maturing teenager who desires to serve, or the college student that may be old enough but not mature enough to serve, create unique discernment parameters for leader selection in the church. I have been placed in a situation where a maturing 17-year-old high school senior was in a better place to lead than a 19-year college sophomore; however, it was still not wise to place the minor in a leadership position. In these ministry situations, they should always serve with a host of adults.

Youth ministry can struggle in this area as high school students desire to be hands-on in ministry by serving in the preschool and children's ministry. First, we want to nurture the older teenager to serve and utilize their gifts for Christ. But we also must consider that these teens are still minors. They cannot be legally considered adult volunteers, which creates a liability concern. So what do you do if you rely on teenagers and young adults to supervise minors? If this is a practice you feel you have to continue, the minor serving should be trained and vetted as much as possible. (Having a background check performed isn't easy or feasible on minors, so you may have to rely on other methods.) But if your church has recruited a minor to serve in leadership, I would advise that you at least make sure that liability issues and safeguards have been established to protect the minors being supervised, the teenager doing the supervising, and the church and ministry as a whole. There is too much at stake to leave anything to chance.

We must think three steps ahead: if a problem were to arise where a teenager was serving, and an accident occurred, or allegation was raised because of the care a child received, how is everyone protected?

    1. KNOW YOUR POLICIES. Consult your local and state laws as well as your insurance provider for staffing ministry with adults and minors to be sure your policies comply. Be sure the background checks and volunteer screening applications are legal and cover the questions and information that your insurance provider recommends.

    2. CONSIDER OUTSIDE TRAINING. Your staff, leaders, and volunteers might benefit from outside training that helps address the importance of vetting your volunteers. We believe in the ministry of MinistrySafe, and highly recommend partnering to address blind spots that have caused great

harm to people, their church, and community. Your ministry associations can also provide resources and training as well as your insurance provider.

If you are a volunteer or paid minister, you may consider the liability protection provided under your home owner's policy or an additional policy to protect your liability while serving in ministry. We never take out an insurance policy that we intend to ever utilize, but in a society where an innocent person can be wrongfully accused, it may be prudent to protect your family as you minister to other families.

The final word is to use common sense as you minister to minors and be sure the volunteers understand this critical component. Many of the unfortunate headlines could have been avoided had someone been held accountable for their walk with the Lord or their behavior with others.

QUESTIONS TO CONSIDER:

1. What systems or safeguards do you need to develop to enhance your process for selecting volunteers?

2. Do you spend time praying over names of possible volunteers and your enlisted leaders? How might you and your team grow in this area?

CHAPTER THREE: MAKING MONEY MATTER

BY DR. JODY DEAN

If you're a youth worker, the following scenario may feel very familiar:

A parent hands you their child's camp deposit on Sunday morning. Later that afternoon, you're playing laser tag with a few of your senior guys. A couple students pay for their own. Between this Sunday and next Sunday, several students and parents drop off envelopes for various fundraisers and events. This is a typical week in the life of a youth worker.

Here's the thing: you think you know exactly what you have been given and feel confident you will be able to sort it out later. But then suddenly it's been a few days before you can get to the pile that has now been stuffed inside your Bible and stacked on your desk and imagine that: the math does not add up. Now what?

Even with the best of intentions, we can mishandle money. As youth workers, we often have multiple financial initiatives going on: money for events, paying the bills on trips, online accounts, petty cash, and fundraisers to name a few. We need guidelines and best practices to help us stay organized and accountable.

Here's a transparent reality: A couple of times early in my ministry, I had to pay a little of my own cash to cover for a missing receipt. I had to make sure that things added up and that I was above board with money in my ministry. This was early on in my career when I served in churches that did not have clear guidelines for money, and I simply did the best that I could. Now, the money was always accurate, and the balance was what it should have been, but the burden of proof was always one me alone. I was accountable, and my word had to suffice.

I have become zealous as I've grown in leadership for maintaining ministry integrity through finances. Student ministries often struggle in this area. This is almost always due to inadequate guidelines and processes.

The privilege of handling financial resources can become a burden due to budgets, designated donations, registration fees, and fundraising. This responsibility is to be taken seriously. Too many youth ministers are casual, careless, or incompetent in the area of stewardship of resources. Lasting damage can happen to the ministry as a result.

In youth ministry, we are always collecting payments for events, trips, camps, or mission trips. These payments have to be handled in an accountable manner to avoid an integrity accusation for the person or ministry. Spreadsheets are your friend only if they are maintained. But organization is just one piece of the pie.

Let's say a student has a sports camp the week of your mission trip, and his parents would like a refund for their fundraising. How do you handle this? Don't wait until you're in this difficult situation to come up with a solution. Know your policies on deposits, cancellations, and who pays for what when. Make sure they are communicated to parents and stick to them.

Speaking of policies and practices, here are some thoughts to consider as you evaluate:

HAVE A SYSTEM SET UP FOR ACCOUNTABILITY
You need a process that will record receipts, donations, and expenditures. A triplicate receipt book for payments and donations is not a bad place to start: one receipt for the person receiving the funds, one for the person that is making the contribution or payment, and then one for your record for the system you have in case the file is lost or has a discrepancy. You can envision the parent who thinks they have paid their balance for their child's trip in full, but your records do not agree. A triplicate receipt can help clarify the problem.

It doesn't matter what you use, as long as you use something. If you do not have a system, then you will be challenged or accused at some point over finances, whether from a specific student or a general integrity accusation due to the overall practices in funding the work.

AVOID A SEPARATE CHECKING ACCOUNT FOR YOUR AREA OF MINISTRY
If possible, process all finances through the church accounting system. Some churches have operated with a separate banking account that exists outside of the primary checking account and offerings of the church. Your liability for this practice is increased, as well as the potential for your integrity to be questioned if someone challenges your spending or accounting.

USE DISCERNMENT WITH PRIVATE DONATIONS
You may from time to time have a church member express the desire to privately donate money directly to your ministry. The best practice in this area is always to consult the financial administrator and pastor before accepting a designated donation for student ministry. Few things are truly free. There could be an expectation for favors or position within your ministry.

FUNDRAISERS CAN BE A BLESSING AND A CURSE
In one church, I seemed to always be focusing on planning the next way to raise enough money to do the ministry and help families. In that same setting, the families seemed to find the money to do the things at school they valued without fundraising, and manpower was being leveraged for fund creation instead of making disciples.

You may envision a great way to raise quick cash, but do what you can to strongly encourage God's people to tithe. Don't take away the blessing it is for church members to give to support the work of their church.

In churches that do not allow fundraisers, an entire layer of administration is removed by not having to keep up with all the details they entail. Of course, each church is different, and you should be wise in the number of fundraisers and the integrity of how those funds are utilized. I am not for or against fundraisers and have been both blessed and cursed in dealing with them. Another consideration in raising funds is that it can become more challenging if your ministry grows. For example, a car wash in a ministry taking 20 to camp can be a great day of fellowship and fund creation. The next year the event with 40 going to camp can be defeating when the fellowship is less because everyone cannot stay busy and the funds created did not equal minimum wage for the day.

In my ministry, fundraising became more difficult as we grew in number, and those giving the funds did not have the bandwidth to provide the per capita dollar amount for each student as we grew. This can also cause your leadership and management to be questioned when families begin paying more than they are accustomed but are involved in the same amount of work and effort as in previous years of fundraisers.

SCHOLARSHIPS SHOULD BE CONSIDERED IN THE SAME MANNER THAT COLLEGES ISSUE FUNDS
One way that funds are awarded is based on need through financial aid. I have never had a youth stay home because I could not find a way to provide the financial aid they needed to be involved in the ministry. In the past, I have even awarded excellence-in-ministry scholarships. You could create a discipleship recognition that rewards those students that accomplish certain goals or other markers of achievement in your ministry.

Many times, we only reserve funds for need and not merit. I believe being able to award a scholarship for a mission trip or camp that reveals ministry excellence can encourage others to strive to be involved. I have been blessed to have a scholarship account in ministry that even at times allowed all to receive some scholarship for the trip. I strived to prioritize the mission opportunities first when funds were available to scholarship students.

CREATE FINANCIAL POLICIES THROUGH THE CHURCH LEADERSHIP STRUCTURE AND A HANDBOOK FOR YOUTH MINISTRY

Schools provide great insight for having a handbook that outlines your weekly ministry schedule, explains the finances including any fundraisers and refunds, chaperone selection, and discipline. A handbook that a student and guardian signs acknowledging their knowledge of the content can help you when a problem arises in your ministry specifically in the area of finances. Emotions get heated quickly with some people when the topic involves money so be sure to safeguard yourself and the youth ministry you have been called to lead.

As we wrap up this section, I believe the biblical example for finances is clear. We are to bring the money to the storehouse. The church creates a budget to execute the vision and mission through the giving of the people. It is my personal belief that youth ministry is a part of the church and not its own entity. Therefore, the finances should be handled as a part of the whole of the church and not through auxiliary funding streams and accounts when possible.

The church should include youth ministry in their ministry spending as other ministries are included in the general operating budget. A youth minister and the volunteers should be tithing to the work at the church and not designated accounts for their ministry. Designated giving instead of a general tithe should not be the only way a person gives to the ministry of the church.

The youth minister should guard against building an area of ministry that does operate under the vision and direction of the church. Although some churches allow for separate checking accounts or fundraising the youth budget to limit the church's burden for teenagers would not be best practices for handling youth ministry finances.

QUESTIONS TO CONSIDER:

1. What are your church's policies on fundraising? Have you found fundraisers to be something that benefits your youth ministry and youth ministry culture? Or have they been a drain? How can you re-think fundraising so that it's a "win-win" for you and students?

2. Does your youth ministry operate within the church's overall financial policy and procedure? If not, how might you begin a discussion to move it there?

3. What improvements do you need to consider in your personal money matters to be more efficient and accountable to the church?

PART 2

SHEPHERDING THE PEOPLE

In this section, the focus is on emotional protection. Part of risk management includes counseling, safety guidelines, and addressing bullying. As a minister, I am sad that these things are necessary to mention in a book intended for church leaders. I pray for discipleship and maturity that removes the need for being cautious in giving spiritual advice with integrity. I wish we didn't have to talk about the possibility of harm coming to students, especially at church. I pray for a better understanding of the worth of every single person who comes into the sphere of our care. Until that day, we pray, we counsel, we protect, and we create a culture that is intolerant to anyone being marginalized.

CHAPTER FOUR: COUNSELING CONSIDERATIONS

BY DR. ALLEN JACKSON

It is ironic that I am writing this chapter just days after I had a counseling conversation in which I blew it. I said too much, told stories that were unnecessary and answered questions that were not being asked. Basically, I made a mess of a conversation where someone wanted to trust me. Maybe I was insecure; maybe I was having a bad day; maybe I was overwhelmed by the situation. Hopefully, I will get a chance to make it right, but you can be comforted in knowing that four decades of doing ministry never makes these conversations any easier.

As a pastor and a professor with experience and education, I still do not have the credentials and training to call what I do "professional counseling." Let me say that another way. Unless you have professional training and professional certification, I think it unwise to schedule counseling sessions as if you were a therapist. Naturally, conversations will occur with people who need spiritual advice. Guidelines concerning these conversations as well as referral skills are necessary.

Youth ministry is about relationships between adults and students. I went back and dusted off some youth ministry notes from my early days at the seminary, and I found a section that is still helpful. There are at least five types of relationships that youth workers can have with students or adults. Imagine someone who needs help (a teenager or a parent or a volunteer) in a boat in a moving river, heading toward a waterfall. You are about to be involved in the situation. You can be:

1. An advice-giver, standing on the shoreline with a megaphone. "Be careful! Get out of there. Can't you see it's dangerous?"
2. A reassuring presence: "Everything will be okay. Help is on the way. I'm here for you."
3. An understanding listener, wading in the water towards the boat. "I know what you are going through. I feel for you."
4. A self-revealer, climbing in the boat with them. "I'm here with you. We

will get through this together. Tell me how you want to get out of this mess, and I will help you."
5. A rescuer, getting in the boat and grabbing a paddle. "Let me do it for you. I'll get us out and then maybe we'll talk about the experience."

Why the parable? Because if we are fulfilling our calling in youth ministry, we will always be in a relationship with students and students tend to have drama in their lives. We want to help with their problems, but we don't want to solve their problems for them. We should not routinely bail them out, and our words are hollow if we are shouting from a distance. At various times, we will be all of the above, yet the optimal relationship to settle on is the self-revealer. Our presence and our trust in a student's ability to think critically about a situation and make a decision is a key to multiplying disciples. When we are in the boat with them, we should make sure the student keeps hold of the paddle!

At the heart of this chapter is the distinction between giving advice as a trusted leader, mentor, and guide and becoming involved with an acute psychological or emotional issue. Most youth pastors provide some level of counseling to students and adults both in the church and in the community. Discernment is critical in knowing when a conversation crosses the line into professional counseling.

RETAIN OR REFER?
Several scenarios might unfold with you as a counselor. You might have a sideline conversation in the youth room or worship space. You might end up talking to a student at an activity like a retreat, or in the bleachers at a ball game. You might get a call from a student or an adult saying, "I really need to talk to you. Can I come to your office?"

A conversation gets started, usually about a problem, a relationship, a decision, or a negative action that appears to have consequences.

As you listen to the initial conversation, you engage in a sort of decision tree. Is the issue a spiritual one? Is anyone in imminent danger? How many people are involved? Does the person need me to comment or do they just need to process verbally? Is this issue within my ability to advise? Do I retain (keep the conversation going in this and future talks) or do I refer (put them in touch with a person better equipped for this issue)?

If you retain—if you decide you are the right person to help in a problem that has come to your attention, then rule number one is to remember that you are the adult (in the case of the student) or the pastor/spiritual guide (in the case of an adult). Your goal is not to be liked or affirmed. Your goal is to speak the truth in love. A secondary goal is to move forward. The mission of the church is to make disciples, and if a person needs to make some adjustments to that end, you are the right one for the conversation.

I like a quote from my co-author, Dr. Jody Dean. In discussing this, he gave me this paragraph:

> Every youth minister should have trustworthy, professional Christian counselors on speed dial. I refer a student, adult volunteer, or parent to a licensed professional counselor once the conversation moves beyond spiritual battles and struggles. It took me years in ministry to learn I could not answer all questions or provide counsel to resolve all of life's issues. The longer my tenure at a church, the more counsel I provided to adults as they also came for advice. So, counseling will require you to have empathy for the struggles an average person deals with during their life, but to know when to call in outside help.

A lot is going on in that quote, all of it wise. If the issue is one requiring confession, repentance, prayer, spiritual discernment, clarity of a future calling, a biblical question or a wrestling with God's will, the conversation belongs in your court as the youth worker. If you are getting to know students and their families as you should be doing, you are aware of context. You understand the family system this student or adult is in. You know that time takes care of many issues, and so you understand that a child becomes a middle schooler who becomes a high schooler who becomes a young adult. You know of resources in the church, programs and support groups to recommend for involvement. You also have the relationships to talk to students and their parents since solutions usually come from a synergy of the generations.

But you also know when you are over your head and it is time to refer. Don't jump to the conclusion that all conversations where your advice is requested are about emotional issues. If someone wants to know if they should enlist in the military, you might refer them to someone who is serving or who has served. If someone needs networking help with a career, you might link them with someone in the field.

Also, don't jump to the conclusion that a referral is necessary because you aren't smart enough, wise enough, trained enough, experienced enough to handle even a very complex issue. Many times, the wise play is to allow a person to see someone else for a variety of reasons. I found a great article entitled, "It's Time to Refer When . . ." by Robert Heiliger who is a pastoral counselor.[7] His view is that the need for referral is not always due to lack of skill (though sometimes it is), but it also may be because a pastor does not have the time to do the counseling properly. Most sources say that if three visits don't move a person forward, then it is time to refer, and if a youth worker begins to see several people in counseling situations, it is likely that other duties are being neglected.

You may realize quickly that the motivation of the person who comes to you for advice is not entirely pure. Sometimes, a person has a different reason for wanting to see you, such as an agenda they want you to help them push or gossip they want to spread or to get you on their side for a conflict. Some persons have a romantic fantasy, and as affirming as it is to be wanted or needed, you need to be aware of boundaries. Heiliger says, "There are spatial boundaries (such as touch or how close people sit), verbal boundaries (such as the appropriateness of words in a social or professional context), and time boundaries (phone calls or appointments at unusual hours) that need to be attended to. Most pastors have good intuitive skills, but we all have a blind spot. Seek peer or professional supervision when it feels funny to you."[8] Good advice.

LAND MINES IN COUNSELING

First, I would recommend that you do not call what you do "counseling." If someone is coming to see you, write their name on your calendar, create a file folder called, "Spiritual Conversations" and let them talk. When you have decided to retain or refer, jot down a few notes about your conversation, put it in your folder and lock it away. It is better that you keep the mindset of a pastor instead of a therapist.

Second, be aware of how these conversations affect you. It is a wonderful thing to be able to help hurting people, but sometimes we should heed the words of Romans 12:3: "For by the grace given me I say to every one of you: Do not think of yourself more highly than you ought, but rather think of yourself with sober judgment, in accordance with the faith God has distributed to each of you." (NIV). It is easy to get caught up in the accolades of "you are so wise and helpful" and lose sight of the goal: discipleship, not your ego.

Thirdly, back to the boundary issues. While the motivation of the person seeking advice might not be pure, it is important for yours to be. You are stepping on a landmine when your private thoughts drift from offering spiritual advice to a romantic relationship. These are the stories of pastors and youth pastors who ended up leaving the ministry in shame due to an affair.

Fourth, remember that confidentiality is absolute, except in a mandatory report situation (see the next section). If you find that you talk about counseling situations with your spouse, your friends, your neighbors or even other pastors, then you should get out of the counseling business. The things you hear are often painful, sometimes shocking and always interesting. Write your notes, lock your folder away and honor the privacy of the person who came to see you. To hear confession is a sacred trust.

To avoid landmines is more than just good advice. Giving advice without the skill to do so is called negligent counseling or malpractice. If it results in injury, you are liable. Sexual misconduct is inexcusable, and youth pastors who engage in sexual misconduct while engaged in a counseling relationship are exposing themselves and their church to potentially significant legal risk, to say nothing of the spiritual ramifications. Too many youth ministers are now in prison because they didn't behave themselves sexually.

FALSE ACCUSATIONS
Rarely, but occasionally, a student or adult might accuse you of misconduct to humiliate or retaliate because of something you have said or done that they found offensive. Because most counseling is done behind closed doors, the possibility of false accusations is real. As I said in the first chapter, your character is your first line of defense for a false accusation. Unfortunately, a false accusation can end your ministry as quickly as one with merit. Use wisdom and use common sense in creating an environment to speak the truth in love.

Here are a few more brief considerations:[9]

AVOID CONTROVERSIAL THERAPIES
Youth pastors should avoid any controversial counseling techniques that have been associated in recent years with staggering levels of liability, specifically in areas like eating disorders, sexual orientation, age regression therapy or multiple personality disorders.

ENSURE YOU AREN'T ALONE IN THE CHURCH WITH ANYONE
A window in your office with an assistant, volunteer, or another staff member immediately outside is a great way to protect from false accusation or inappropriate activity.

BLUE ON BLUE, PINK ON PINK
In many cases, I will not counsel a female alone if the conversation involves more than prayer without my wife in the room. Some churches have adopted this as policy. If possible, let women counsel women. This might be someone on the staff or a referral.

QUESTIONS TO CONSIDER:
1. As a youth worker, how often do you find yourself in a counseling situation with a student or volunteer? How well do you feel that you are equipped to be having these conversations?

2. Do you ever have mentoring encounters with students that turn toward counseling? How do you handle these transitions?

3. What safeguards or protocols do you have informally or formally for counseling a student and when to refer someone for a licensed Christian counselor?

CHAPTER FIVE: PRACTICING PROTECTIVE PROCEDURES

BY DR. JODY DEAN

In days gone by, youth workers (including both authors of this book) did stupid things.

What epic adventures do you recall as you think back through events, games, and memories of youth ministry? You may want to pause now and pray while breathing a sigh of relief that you survived.

I have an epic top ten. These ministry stories seem to grow like the ones my grandfather used to tell about his childhood. Each time a former student reminds me of something we did at an event, it triggers this sigh of relief and awkward laughter all at the same time. How did I (and my students) survive those moments?

I remember a youth event in the seventh grade that involved a hatchback with seven students and five seatbelts. A routine traffic stop provided an epic story of six boys laughing at the youth minister being asked to step out of the car. However, the days of an officer saying, "be safe and don't do this again," have evolved to social media videos, lost credibility, and even jail time. (Now, you don't need me to tell you this, but this type of social media attention isn't the kind you want. The type of social media identity you want to be cultivating is one based on common sense and protective actions in everything from the icebreaker kickoff game on Wednesday evening to how you transport students to host homes during a DNow. But I digress.)

The ease with which information is captured and transmitted has created a culture of instant accountability. Winning coaches are fired due to a lapse in judgment during practice toward a player. Award-winning teachers have a bad day in the classroom, and because it's captured on video, they lose tenure. Leaders abuse the authority of their office, emails are leaked, and their careers are over. The ability to capture a pic or video and share with a mass audience has created a layer of accountability that requires extra diligence in how we lead and guard the ministry.

If an activity during your weekly schedule or at a retreat is questionable, then you and any volunteers may have to answer questions with parents and leaders in the church. Youth ministry needs to guard and protect students from initiation into your ministry during their small group or at camp. Some churches are large enough that middle and high school students are divided, but the inappropriate behavior to the youngest in the dorm at camp or during Wednesday night may still occur in the separate groups.

While fun is important (this is youth ministry, after all), the main focus of your ministry should be on reaching and making disciples, not creating legendary stories. While we can reminisce about the freewheeling days of youth ministry's past, the truth is that the level of scrutiny given to making sure we protect those we've been entrusted with is a positive development.

As you begin to think about the types of procedures that will help protect your ministry, take a moment and give the following considerations some thought:

PAY ATTENTION TO ALL ASPECTS OF A GAME
Games are a part of youth ministry. They create community and provide an environment for youth to strengthen relationships. They are an essential aspect of your weekly worship or event. But simple games can turn into a train wreck when someone gets hurt because things got out of control, or someone gets humiliated and leaves your youth ministry as a result.

Consider all aspects of a game before you decide to use it in your ministry: socio-economic status of those participating, gender, age-range, what your students might be wearing, any physical limitations, and so in. The best-planned game can still fail. Have a transition or backup plan. When a game does not work as planned, learn from the experience and be better prepared in the future. A game that causes a teenager anxiety or distress should be eliminated. If a game unexpectedly results in an outcome you feel may put a teenager in an awkward position, you should reach out to the family and engage in conversation, especially if you were a participant.

Games serve a useful purpose in your overall ministry. But because they have the possibility of risk, they shouldn't be entered into without some thought. Games shouldn't be a last-minute time filler because you had little preparation time for Wednesday night. And they should never be the focus of what you do.

REMOVE DISTRACTIONS
Often, students who aren't engaged in your activities are the ones who end up getting in trouble. Keeping all of your students engaged in activities, Bible study, worship, and events can be a challenge. But protecting your students from outside distractions can help in keeping the student engaged.

Smartphones and social media allow them to be present but still connected to peers that are not attending. Technology has created the allusion of presence with students, but many times they are not engaged in the time you are sharing at church. But you can foster intentionality and engagement by having a social media policy and smartphone parameters each week in your gatherings. You can even create opportunities to utilize technology in your group by messaging friends not present, inviting friends to an event, or utilize the note feature to engage in the application of the teaching.

The hardest students to engage are the loners or disengaged students, usually because of forced attendance, who have the attitude that if you speak to them, they will either be hostile or disregard you completely. However, the students that are disengaged and do not have community can be the students that need an adult to invest in them and unearth what is happening in their lives.

TAKE INTO CONSIDERATION HOW TO ENGAGE STUDENTS WITH LEARNING DISABILITIES AND SPECIAL NEEDS

As you consider your programming, you must take into consideration students in your ministry that have special needs. You want to create a safe space for these students to grow in discipleship and community. Students with special needs want to participate, but sometimes can't due to the challenges of the way we program. For instance, maybe you have planned an ice-breaker that is chaotic or loud. This may be especially challenging for students in your ministry who have special needs. They may not be able to engage because the activities or games that are planned do not have considerations for their physical or mental challenges, and therefore reduces their ability to participate. The last thing you want is for a student with special needs to merely be a spectator of your ministry and not a participant.

Each student in your ministry should be considered in your planning process. Now, not every activity you do may allow for accommodation or modification for inclusion. But mindfulness of these students and their needs should be your overarching goal. Have conversations with parents and let them know you how much you value their child's involvement. Assure parents that you will create as many ways as possible for their student to be protected and engaged in the ministry.

PAY ATTENTION TO WHAT YOUR STUDENTS ARE DOING

It's often the little things that create the most risk. Attention to detail is a learned skill, but one that goes a long way toward mitigating risk in your ministry. Want an example? Seatbelts.

Seatbelts may seem like an obvious detail when transporting adolescents, but each time I drive a church vehicle, I have to remind everyone from children to senior adults to buckle up. A detail that will trip you up every time is making sure you have a seat with a seat belt for every person that needs to be transported. It's an attention to detail that saves lives.

In general, car safety is a huge point of emphasis in risk management, and it's not just seatbelts. I remember discovering a group of guys hood surfing on a vehicle in the parking lot, which of course abruptly came to a halt. In general, as you seek to manage the risk in your ministry, make sure the students in your care are abiding by the law, whether they have a driver's license or not.

IF IN DOUBT, TALK TO YOUR INSURANCE PROVIDER

Many activities that have been a part of youth ministry for years have to be considered for their risk factor and overall impact in today's culture. Few activities are viewed through the lens of whether or not they aid in accomplishing the vision and mission of the church, specifically related to youth ministry. Memories of hood sledding in a field, a homemade zip line, or extreme weekends in the outdoors are some examples of events that are fun but may not contribute to your overall goals for your ministry.

If an activity or event holds some inherent risk (skiing, ropes courses, etc.) but is an essential part of your ministry design, then consult your insurance provider for a special event policy to provide additional liability coverage. Also, these types of events are not for everyone, and you need to consider all students as you plan. You need a leadership team that will help you diversify your events to be sure all teenagers have things they can be involved in that address their needs, interests, and learning styles.

YOU MUST ADDRESS AND REPORT ANY ILLEGAL ACTIONS

If there is anything we've learned in our current culture, it's that you must report any illegal or potentially illegal actions by an adult or student. (There is a much more in-depth section on this in Chapter 8. See this is an introduction to the topic.) You are a minister, not a detective. If you observe or suspect illegal activity, you have an ethical obligation to report it to the proper authorities. Deflecting, looking the other way, or taking the "kids will be kids" approach of many parents may be the easier path, but illegal activities must be handled as prescribed by the law. This as much as anything is a practice that is foundational to practicing protective procedures.

What does this look like? I'm not a lawyer and procedures will vary depending on your local or state laws. You'll want to do further research to make sure you comply. But at the minimum, it is a wise practice to have a file with dates, time, people involved, and steps taken to address the situation and to make this information available to your senior leadership as well as law enforcement.

How you handle the situation moving forward is a delicate discussion. There is the need to minister to those involved, but the nature of the situation may dictate various courses of action. You have to shepherd and protect the entirety of your ministry. The best advice is to work with your church's leadership to determine the right way to move forward in a situation where you have to report illegal activity.

As a minister, my default position is grace, but I also have relationships with lawyers and police officers to understand the law. These men and women are also helpful in providing insight into new harmful developments within the community at large.

QUESTIONS TO CONSIDER:

1. What aspects of your ministry struggles to engage all teenagers into your event, their small group, or worship time?

2. How do you evaluate activities, games, or interactive experiences for various categories of appropriateness?

3. How can you limit outside influences through texting and social media while students are gathered for your ministry?

4. How comfortable are you with the rules and guidelines about reporting illegal or questionable activity? What can you and your team do to be come more knowledgeable in this area?

CHAPTER SIX: OWNING ONLINE OBNOXIOUSNESS

BY DR. JODY DEAN

Do you struggle with a framework for interacting with students through technology while being above reproach in the process? All three aspects of shepherding fit this topic: protecting, examining, and guiding youth and volunteers in their social media practices. Most adults understand they should not have a private chat, text, or message through social media with just one student. Many times, these encounters with an adult and student happen by accident, or because a framework for these types of interaction does not exist.

Stories abound of youth ministers taking a student home with no other adult in the car, or of a one-on-one counseling session happening with no accountability, or of an interaction with the student who hangs back to talk when no another adult or teenager is around. Ministers and volunteers alike recognize these as problematic situations. Many of us know the importance of accountability in this area and know how to have private conversations and still have visibility and accountability. But social media seems to be an area where we can easily lose track of the safeguards we'd otherwise put in place. How do we manage these situations?

Before we jump into a discussion of risk management and social media, I want first to stop and address social media behavior, specifically what I call online obnoxiousness. Social media has led to an increase in connectivity between people, but that comes with a lot of information that is shared as a result. Online people can be stalked, praised, harassed, humiliated, self-promoted, and informed. People can be harassed and shamed online even worse than if it had happened in front of their entire school. They can be rude, unaware, happy, transparent, and lonely even though they are connected to numerous people in online activity.

Teenagers, parents, and youth volunteers must learn boundaries for their posting, sharing, and revealing personal details. Social media is a valuable tool in youth ministry as it allows a youth ministry to be connected more than ever, sharing truth and potentially taking interactions deeper than may happen while in another's physical presence. But we have to be careful. School districts and employers are implementing social media policies. Consider creating one for your church and youth ministry. It's important to be able to answer the question: is your church liable if negative behavior begins through a church connection and moves to the social media realm?

Non-verbal communication can be misconstrued quickly. You may have had a texting conversation that went a direction of someone interpreting your statements in a way that you did not intend. Many times, our social media posts can lead to miscommunication. Factors such as a lack of body language or tone of voice make these kinds of conversations murky and complicated.

Online obnoxiousness moves beyond the annoying person who shares too many images, comments, or details. It's about the person who is demeaning, derogatory, or abusive in their communication. This type of behavior usually happens through private messaging via text or another communication app, where inappropriate behavior can wreck lives. Youth ministry must help teenagers, parents, and youth volunteers protect their lives and learn media practices that nurture spiritual maturity with the goal of a holistic lifestyle of representing Christ.

Teenagers are finding ways to chat online, connect online, game online, and also make sinful mistakes online. They are more connected than any generation before them. They are digital natives; they have always had an online mechanism to find people or information. Since adults have been learning at the same time as children, many are behind the curve in what is available to teenagers in social media. It is incredible to see how people "remove the gloves" in their online public communication as they post their unfiltered thoughts, opinions, and frustrations toward a person, organization, or position. I have developed a few considerations as you try to tackle the behemoth of online obnoxiousness.

Here are some thoughts to help you as you think about how to address the social media behaviors of your ministry and the people surrounding and surrounding your ministry:

ALWAYS TEXT IN A GROUP
Many people don't think twice about texting an adult volunteer, regardless of gender. But I would suggest that it's wise to never text an adult leader without including a third person for accountability. I always text in a group if possible. (If you can figure out ways to group text without everyone replying OK to the group when a response is not needed, then please text me your solution.)

The same principle is valid for teenagers. Additionally, when texting with teenagers, always keep the text to ministry. If the texting becomes personal, then safeguard by moving to end the communication. If you discover a student is in crisis, you need to have a safe plan to deal with the situation in a manner beyond text counseling.

MOST ADULTS USE SOCIAL MEDIA IN A DIFFERENT WAY THAN STUDENTS

Many parents and youth workers appear to be using social media primarily as a way to stay in touch with family and friends. Social media is becoming the new "family or class reunion" for adults, a place to share pictures with family and friends, and have a broader audience to share life events. Teenagers, on the other hand, use social media as a means to keep chatting and hanging out like many adults use to do by being together in physical space and not just online.

If you're like me, you may remember when your family got a 25ft cord for the phone, and you could then extend from beyond the kitchen to a nearby room for more privacy. (I know I just dated myself.) You can then remember the invention of a cordless phone that became another game changer, before the bag phone in the car and ultimately the smartphone. Teenagers today are not only utilizing texting, social media, and live game streams to communicate with each other, they even have the technology to remove these conversations, so no one knows they even had correspondence with people. The days of Mom reading their diary or listening at the door has been eliminated. A teenager dealing with online obnoxiousness may not tell an adult because they were not supposed to be online themselves. The result may be the teenager refrains from sharing about the negative hating, stalking, or abusive behavior through an online connection.

TECH-SAVVY DOESN'T EQUAL MATURE

Private chat apps and live chat sites create a screen name that allows for communication with people that a teenager may not even know. Teenagers can be naive in their online behavior and connections by assuming the people they chat and share information with are the person their screen name and information portrays. As adults, we understand that online behavior includes twisted people who prey on victims to accomplish their own sick and sinful desires. Teenagers are private chatting to eliminate a trail of communication because just like a teenager would hide their diary, they are finding ways to remove information so that adults cannot read their messages.

A parent and youth volunteer needs to be aware of the resources available and how they work. Also, parents and youth volunteers need to be equipped on how to create accountable ways that will aid in keeping their teenager from being targeted in obnoxious online behavior. The reverse is also true, and that would be to help teenagers not create or engage in obnoxious online behavior.

THERE'S ALWAYS MORE TO KNOW

The story of social media is still being written because hundreds of sites, options, and apps have been created since the introduction of Myspace. New ways will always continue to be designed for teenagers and adults to interact. These options will only become more advanced with more features for diverse connectivity and ways to interact. As you navigate youth culture in your ministry, it should include the online components your students are engaged with. Discern how to mediate obnoxious behavior from occurring within your teenagers and ministry. If your ministry pushes teenagers to online options, you need to safeguard that connection.

HELP BUILD A FILTER

Landing the helicopter for online behavior is not easy because the Internet is scarier than we care to admit. Teenagers have committed suicide, dealt with depression, and withdrawn from people due to obnoxious online behavior. The reality is that unguarded apps and social media can take teenagers to places we do not intend for them to go. Adults may have greater discernment in their online behavior; however, students have a limited filter. Although this may be assumed, as an adult you should not be instigating or contributing to obnoxious online behavior. Interaction among teenagers or teenagers with adults can enter into illegal activity and should be guarded.

QUESTIONS TO CONSIDER:

1. What metrics do you have to gauge online social interactions of people engaged in your ministry as a teenager, parent, or youth worker?

2. How can you teach and inform teenagers, parents, and youth workers about obnoxious behavior?

3. Does your youth ministry or church have a social media and internet policy?

4. Does your ministry utilize social media and texting? If so, how do you utilize these connections and how are you protecting students within them?

CHAPTER SEVEN: BURSTING THE BULLYING BALLOON

BY DR. JODY DEAN

At some point, most of us have been on the receiving end of a painful putdown. Whether it's aimed at our height, weight, skin color, gender, or academic abilities, the one-liner is synonymous with bullying. I remember careless comments from days of wearing husky Levi's before my height and width balanced out. Most of us learn to deal with these remarks. However, the current climate of extremes in our culture leads many teenagers to avoid seeing the harm in their actions toward others.

Increasingly, youth ministers are aware of bullying directed toward students for many reasons. Younger students are bullied as an act of "hazing." A less advantaged student is bullied because they don't have the right clothes. More popular students might tease or exclude or bully a teen that is not as socially "in." I want to encourage you to minister to the bully and those that are bullied. When you consider a bully's life, a sin issue needs attention or at best an internal struggle that is being acted out in real ways toward others.

"Boys will be boys," some might say, dismissing teasing, bullying, and peer pressure as inevitable behavior among many adolescent and pre-adolescent boys. But we know that this painful set of relentless practices sanctioned by the boy culture and laughed off by many well-meaning parents and teachers falls along a continuum of boys abusing each other, a slippery slope that ranges from verbal taunts to physical threats to sheer (and sometimes lethal) violence."[10]

"Girls will be girls," some might say, dismissing girl drama, hurtful exchanges, or cliques as inevitable behavior among many adolescent and preadolescent girls. According to the National Education Association, approximately 160,000 children miss school every day due to fear of attack or intimidation by other students. Also, every seven minutes a child is bullied and over one million children deal with cyberbullying.[11] Parents, volunteers, and ministers should consider teasing and bullying in your ministry as a serious issue that needs a clear plan for ministering to bullies and their victims.

I was bullied my entire seventh-grade year at church to the extent I desired to stop attending. The ongoing "initiation" was a challenge for me. Unfortunately, most leadership thought the situation was funny and did not wish to intervene. At the time, I thought leadership did not care about me and my well-being, but today I understand it was just their immaturity in ministry leadership. My mother intervened by talking with church leadership, resulting in a change in behavior, and the initiation ceased. However, the experience resulted in my absence from camp that year as well as other aspects of disengagement, ultimately leading to a lack of desire to attend church altogether. While my experience was mild, it still leaves an imprint. Youth leaders should shepherd and protect the students God gives to the ministry and safeguard any teenager from bullying or any signs of social mistreatment.

Bullying has moved to an extreme level that can not only be destructive but even criminal. Youth ministry should be an escape from this type of youth culture. Unfortunately, youth groups can have these fractions among the people that gather each week. I encourage you to reach out and speak truth to your teenagers, volunteers, and parents. The story of the Good Samaritan by Jesus is an excellent illustration of how we should care for one another.

It should be noted that, if you observe or know of any bullying that is abusive (either physically, mentally, or emotionally), you must take steps to report these behaviors to the proper authorities. There is, of course, spiritual growth that can happen within a bullying situation, but students who do not feel safe in your ministry will not be made to feel safe if the only solutions we are offering are spiritual. Some victims of bullying recover over time from the experiences that cause them grief and trauma, but others do not. Students who are bullied are more likely to experience depression, anxiety, health complaints, decreased academic achievements, substance abuse, and in some cases suicide.[12] We must address the root problem of bullying in our ministries because these behaviors have no place in the church.

If we intervene appropriately, redemptive work can occur with the student being bullied in teaching him or her how to overcome struggles and develop perseverance. Those who bully can experience redemption when the sin issues in their lives are revealed and dealt with.

The youth ministry can benefit from learning to share burdens during struggles like a bullying situation: how can youth workers make the group aware of the shared burden of allowing, observing, enabling or not reporting this type of behavior? Galatians shares that the bully will not prosper because "what a person sows he also will reap." However, the challenge for the victim is struggling to display fruits of the Spirit during a difficult encounter. Responding to bullies with love, patience, and kindness can be difficult for the Christian. A good reminder for us in ministry is that all attendees are not Christians and a bullied non-Christian will have a hard time embracing Christ as Savior if they are bullied at church.

Bullying can take on many forms with girl-to-girl drama or guy-to-guy initiation — emotional breakdowns, lines in the sand over friendships, break-ups, towel fights that became more than just camp humor. All of us have experiences with situations that impact teenagers as they make choices, but bullying takes these questions to a different level.

Bullying can also be when a girl bullies a guy, or a guy bullies a girl. These situations can become criminal at a quicker pace than the other issues. You need to be aware of the bad break-ups or stalking relationships and be an advocate for victims. Dating violence and sexual harassment are not issues to be shrugged off as teenage hormones and flirting. As ministers, we must be proactive in protecting the teenagers under our ministry. We all have observed a joke that just went bad and was not intended to harm but escalated in the heat of the moment. These are one-time reparable mistakes and can serve as excellent teaching moments. However, you need to be sure these are unique events and not ongoing bullying of peers.

Bullying ranges from cliques, social hierarchy, gossip, making threats, teasing, cyberbullying, power plays, dating, drugs, exclusionary tactics, partying, and so much more. I pray that these issues do not rise to a level of abuse, but you need to be prepared to refer a student to counseling if needed or be willing to report behavior that is suspicious. Parents cannot become helicopter parents and prevent anything from happening with their teenager, and the same is true for youth ministry. During adolescence, teens have cultural messages that help shape the narrative of how they should look and behave. The lives of our students then evolve according to these standards, because socially they are ruled by this hierarchy. Bullying can then enter into this space where the rules are often invisible or unwritten. These rules can be blurred and broken, and then the enforcement of the rules is not clear. Girls dealing with drama to feel better in the mirror or boys trying to become tough or cool should never rise to the level of harm to a peer.

Youth ministers, leaders, and volunteers should not be instigators for bullying or inappropriate joking that can lead to bullying. I have seen grown men and women revert to the bullying ways of their high school years and incite others. I hope you are not a part of tearing others down, but building them up and making disciples in your ministry. A joke is only fun when everyone is laughing or when everyone is encouraged. The person who is bullied may laugh because they desire to fit in. When adults are involved in bullying, you need to remember the laws adults must adhere to for protecting a minor. If the interaction becomes criminal, the church, ministers, and volunteers may be sued, or charges brought against them. Encourage your leaders to create safe spaces within your ministry where bullying from any source is just not tolerated. Setting an example and modeling this behavior yourself will forge an environment where students feel they are pursued and loved by the people in your church.

All the families in your church are not the same and have different filters and lenses for how they view the issues we are discussing in this chapter. We have blended families, adopted children, foster care, divorce, and nuclear families, to name a few. Also, birth order, gender, age, and other development factors create a melting pot of perspective among adults and teenagers in your church. You could poll three people and get a different answer on whether a single episode or event reached the level of bullying. The challenge is to be diligent to stop bullying and protect teenagers so that the mission of reaching and making disciples is not thwarted.

You may need to develop a policy that deals with parameters and addresses what will be the plan of action for any bullying that occurs in your ministry. Counseling may be needed if you discover an ongoing bullying issue and you may have to report that issue to others. Some warning signs can be found at www.stopbullying.gov

Some of these signs I have observed in youth ministry:
- unexplainable injuries
- lost or destroyed clothing books, electronics, or jewelry,
- frequent headaches or stomachaches
- changes in eating habits
- difficulty sleeping or frequent nightmares
- declining grades, loss of interest in school work, or not wanting to go to school
- sudden loss of friends or avoidance of social situations
- feelings of helplessness or decreased self-esteem
- self- destructive behaviors such as running away from home, harming themselves, or talking about suicide[13]

As ministers, leaders of youth ministry, and parents of teenagers we must become a shepherd that observes the environment so we can protect teenagers that are being and bullied and find ways to reach the instigators with the gospel.

QUESTIONS TO CONSIDER:

1. Honestly assess yourself and your ministry: do you take things too far or instigate inappropriate behavior that could lead to bullying as a leader?

2. Take account of the teenagers at your church. Does anyone have signs of being bullied? What can you do to help them and the bully?

3. How do you monitor the girl drama and issues? How do you monitor the guys and their cutting up or rambunctious behavior?

PART 3

THE SHEPHERD AS AN OVERSEER

The whole concept of "mandatory reporting" sounds ominous. In fact, this entire section is a bit of a downer. We buried it in the book on purpose because if a youth worker reads this first, they might flee from student ministry altogether! This section is a little like buying insurance. You hope you never need it, but it is essential to have it.

The chapter on mandatory reporting is a rather "legalese" sounding discussion on the obligation to report abuse by those of us who work with students or children. We hope we never need it, but it is vital. The second chapter covers the need to have plans for emergencies—or even just unexpected circumstances. We hope we never need it, but it provides clarity in a crisis. A discussion of paperwork and policy is sort of a snoozer, but it provides a road map for the mundane so that you can focus on relationships and spiritual formation that are the heart of student ministry.

Keeping a watch over students and property is like the city wall in biblical cities. It protects and encloses, and you are a bit like the watchman, anticipating trouble areas so that folks in our ministry do not have to. You wish you didn't have to pay attention to these areas, but one of the shepherd's jobs is to keep the sheep safe.

CHAPTER EIGHT: MASTERING MANDATORY REPORTING

BY DR. ALLEN JACKSON

Unfortunately, the scenario is familiar. At a camp, in your office, after a Bible study, or when taking a student home after youth group, you hear something you wish you had not heard. A student tells you that either currently or in their past, they were abused physically, sexually, or emotionally by an adult. Often the adult is a parent or other relative. Equally often, the adult is known by you and other people in your church. Who do you tell? Do you tell anyone? The answer is always "yes."

Every state, the District of Columbia, American Samoa, Guam, the Northern Mariana Islands, Puerto Rico, and the U.S. Virgin Islands have statutes that identify persons who are required to report child maltreatment under specific circumstances.[14] More than half of the states and territories specifically identify ministers as mandatory reporters. This means that if child abuse or neglect is suspected, a youth minister may face criminal charges for remaining silent. Some states exempt pastors and youth pastors who hear about such abuse in a time or place (for example your office) where confidentiality is usually assumed. (The court has in mind the Catholic confessional.) Even if confidentiality exemptions could apply, the moral obligation to protect students remains. Our desire to protect the sheep should be primary.

States that include clergy as mandated reporters are Alabama, Alaska, Arizona, Arkansas, California, Colorado, Connecticut, Georgia, Illinois, Louisiana, Maine, Massachusetts, Michigan, Minnesota, Mississippi, Missouri, Montana, Nevada, New Hampshire, New Mexico, North Dakota, Ohio, Oregon, Pennsylvania, South Carolina, Vermont, West Virginia, and Wisconsin. In approximately 18 States (Delaware, Florida, Idaho, Indiana, Kentucky, Maryland, Mississippi, Nebraska, New Hampshire, New Jersey, New Mexico, North Carolina, Oklahoma, Rhode Island, Tennessee, Texas, Utah, and Wyoming) and Puerto Rico, any person who suspects child abuse or neglect is required to report it. Three of these states (Mississippi, New Hampshire, and New Mexico) specifically identify clergy as mandated reporters. If you are wondering how your state handles ministers as mandatory reporters, a helpful chart is provided at www.childwelfare.gov[15]

If you happen to be reading this book and you are not in the United States, few countries appear to have mandatory reporting laws covering child abuse. The USA, Australia, and Canada are the leading countries that pursue this as an approach, although a range of other countries including Argentina, Sweden, Denmark, Finland, Israel, Kyrgyzstan, the Republic of Korea, Rwanda, Spain, and Sri Lanka have been identified as adopting some form of mandatory reporting legislation. Nonetheless, voluntary reporting systems are considered to be much more common.[16]

Generally speaking, mandatory laws disclosing abuse or intent to harm have to do with harm or neglect of either children or elders. It isn't lost on me that Jesus had much to say about taking care of widows (implied elderly) and orphans (children). Some states require disclosure if you perceive or hear that physical harm to others is likely. There are no federal laws that require you to report it if you hear a student vocalize suicidal thoughts, but each state has its laws on whether reporting is required. Some states also require that parents be notified of a minor's suicidal threats.[17]

I told you it was scary. The bottom line is that we are called to ministry because we want people to thrive physically, mentally, socially, emotionally, and especially spiritually. A student who carries the burden of current or past abuse, a student who wrestles with thoughts of suicide, and a student who intends to harm others cannot be described as thriving. Whether or not we are mandated to report, we have a moral and spiritual obligation to introduce real help to crises. If we have a reasonable belief that abuse occurred or that harm to self or others is imminent, we should call the police or child services. Skip to the end of the chapter if you need the "how to report" guidelines now.

WHEN TO REPORT

Human nature may lead a person to want to deny that abuse is occurring because it is unpleasant. When we know the family of a student who has revealed that they have been or are being hurt, we anticipate the drama that will unfold with reporting. Lives will be altered, families may be separated, a friend or church leader may face legal charges. A person might be reluctant to come forward unless he or she has indisputable evidence of abuse. In many cases, we have only the story told to us by a student, unless physical marks are visible. It is uncomfortable and messy to discern when we should report either our suspicions or what we have heard from a student.

The U.S. Department of Health and Human Services indicates that the following behaviors may signal the presence of abuse: the child will show sudden changes in behavior or school performance, is always watchful, as though preparing for something bad to happen, lacks adult supervision, is overly compliant, passive or withdrawn, comes to school or activities early and does not want to return home, or is reluctant to be around a particular person.[18] There are many other indicators that could also be signs of emotional or physical abuse to a child.

Reporting laws require disclosure when there is "reasonable cause," or a reason to believe that abuse is occurring. This is hard if you suspect that a student is angry at a parent or is seeking attention. If I feel a report or intervention is necessary, I usually bounce the situation (in hypothetical terms, no names) with people I trust like counselors, pastors, or advisors. It is best to talk to people who aren't in your church if you just need advice.

After considering all the factors of which you are aware, and you feel there is reasonable cause, make the call. If you are still on the fence, seek legal advice from a lawyer or child services professional. Many states require that the report is made within 48 to 72 hours after hearing about abuse or neglect. Though we cannot help but be concerned about the complications that will unfold if the accusation is false, from a moral and spiritual standpoint, we have to default on the side of helping a student. From a legal perspective, all states provide protection from litigation against you if a report proves to be false but was made in good faith.[19]

Regardless if you decide to report or if you choose not to report, take notes. After the conversation with a student is over, and you feel like you have either helped them or referred them to someone who can, jot down the details of the conversation and put it in a locked file cabinet. Describe the incident, circumstance and your recollection of the student's story. Your notes may be helpful in the future if the situation escalates or if the church is involved in legal action stemming from the incident. Keep your notes confidential–share them only with those who have a "need to know." You should respect confidentiality and sharing private information could even open you up to a later claim of defamation or invasion of privacy.

[NOTE: We've done our best to provide the most up to date information about the legal considerations concerning reporting. But you should familiarize yourself with the most current policies concerning reporting as there is the very real possibility that guidelines have changed between the time this book was written and when you are reading it.]

ENLIGHTEN VOLUNTEERS

Aside from buying lots of copies of this helpful book and distributing them to everyone you know, you should train other persons who work with youth or children in your church (or school or ministry). Gather a team of people (social workers, ministers, teachers, attorneys) who can help draft policies and procedures for understanding when and how to report. Then stress the importance of following the guidelines. As you will read in a couple of chapters, it is better not to have a policy than to have a policy that is not followed. Try to stay on top of changing legal requirements by educating your team to keep their antenna up.

HOW DO YOU REPORT?

You have decided that a situation warrants disclosure. The Child Welfare Information

Gateway (Children's Bureau in the U.S. Department of Health and Human Services), (www.childwelfare.gov) is helpful to gather information about reporting, but it is not the place to file a report or to receive crisis counseling. Childhelp is a national organization that provides crisis assistance and other counseling and referral services. As of this writing, their hotline is available 24 hours a day, seven days a week, with professional crisis counselors who have access to a database of emergency, social service, and support resources. All calls are anonymous. Contact them at 1.800.4.A.CHILD (1.800.422.4453).[20]

While national hotlines can give you the numbers to call, you still have to call your local child protective services office or law enforcement agency so professionals can assess the situation. Many states have a toll-free number for reporting suspected child abuse or neglect. Even locally, your call is anonymous, and the law enforcement or child protection person on the other end of the line will hopefully (and prayerfully) respond with wisdom and discretion.

Jesus drew children to Himself because of His love, protection, and nurturing spirit. When Jesus' disciples tried to keep children from coming to Jesus, He rebuked them and welcomed the children to His side, saying, "Let the little children come to me and do not hinder them for the kingdom of God belongs to such as these" (Mark 10:14). Then He took the children in His arms and blessed them (verse 16). We can never forget that in Jesus anyone who has abused or has been abused can find hope and forgiveness.

QUESTIONS TO CONSIDER:

    1. Abuse is a real-life issue for many, how do you handle any suspicion or allegations?

    2. What resources do you have in your area to help a victim once you have made a mandatory report to authorities?

    3. How can you begin in your youth ministry become more aware of possible abused teenagers?

CHAPTER NINE: SUPERVISION, SURVEILLANCE, & SECURITY

BY DR. JODY DEAN

"Why"? This is the typical question when I bring up these three "S" words to churches and ministers. "Why do we need security?" "Surveillance? That feels out of place in a church environment." And yet, when articles titled, "Sex offenders groom churches" or "Church seeks to develop U.S.'s first church police department," then my response is that supervision, surveillance, and security are topics we have to at least begin to dialogue. Let me start the conversation by framing some areas that are worth considering.

Cameras, parking lot security, distribution of adult volunteers, and adequate supervision are areas in which the youth ministry has to be diligent to protect students and adults. Supervision is critical when working in a ministry that involves minors. Teenagers do not need to be idle without accountability for their actions. Supervision should include unscheduled hangout times in the youth room, special events, scheduled ministry, and off-site events or retreats. "He said/she said" encounters often end poorly, and when a problem arises, accountable supervision is crucial. The legal system relies on evidence and witnesses when a crime occurs.

Surveillance has many components in youth ministry. Embracing the buddy system, considering your volunteer to student ratio, providing adults who patrol the facilities, and if possible, installing audio/video equipment are all options for surveillance in your ministry. You should never solely rely on technology or one volunteer to be your surveillance for the ministry, but a combination of surveillance that reinforces your supervision. These policies should be followed to not only protect your people and ministry but to safeguard you from negligence and ultimately prevent harm to students.

Security is something teenagers are accustomed to in the society at large. Teenagers and their parents are used to someone in uniform at the theatre, a resource officer at school, and uniform patrols at athletic events they attend. Supervision of their activities at organized venues, surveillance on the school bus or in the hallways, and security on duty at the athletic event or movie theatre are common for teenagers in their weekly routines and activities. Youth ministry and youth volunteers should consider supervision, surveillance, and security during your weekly ministry and special events.

Here are some specific considerations when it comes to this topic:

AN AUDIO/VIDEO SYSTEM IS YOUR FRIEND
Video capture with audio is more affordable than ever. Consider supervision through surveillance as part of your ministry security plan. Many school districts have invested in audio/video recording on buses and classrooms to protect both the employee and children. The church should begin to consider adding an audio/video surveillance system for the perimeter, halls, classrooms, and youth space. Your church may have to take steps to be able to purchase a system depending on budget and size.

The ability to keep an eye on the entire ministry at once is more than a minister or volunteer can accomplish. A video does not lend itself to interpretation if a student denies the account. Many youth ministers have experienced the conversation with a parent who was questioning the facts to what happened concerning their student. If video recording and surveillance is not possible in your ministry setting, then have enough volunteers so the ministry, students, and volunteers are all protected.

ENLIST YOUR VOLUNTEERS
Surveillance through assigned volunteers that walk and patrol the space and grounds can be an excellent aspect to having a watchful eye. Even if you have a good audio/video system, the system does not replace people, and you still need adequate volunteer ratios with students for your ministry. A 5:1 student to volunteer ratio is good practice for investing in student's lives and also keeping an eye on the group. Many times, a student stands alone, and we get busy in the noise and movement of everyone. Volunteers are the key component to keeping an eye on the group so these situations can be addressed.

SECURITY ISN'T JUST A UNIFORM AND A BADGE
Training your volunteers to be strategic and aware of what to look for and protect is an essential aspect of serving. Many churches are adding a security ministry team of volunteers, and the youth ministry should be considered a vital part of that security plan. The church leadership should address insurance provider considerations in protecting security volunteers. A paid, off-duty police officer can be a needed component for safeguarding the entire ministry of the church. Of course, this is only one step and depending on your church size and budget, could get costly.

DON'T BE A COVER
Some students use the church as a cover for doing other things, so the possibility of students arriving and disappearing even if checked-in should be considered in

a patrol plan for the parking lot and building. As students discover their identity and explore freedom, the youth ministry can become a cover for their exploration. They share with their parents they are driving to church but decide to hang out with friends or other activities. In an upcoming chapter, we will outline ways you can create a check-in and check-out process so that the ministry is not easily used as a cover for the teenager's social life.

KNOW YOUR PHYSICAL SURROUNDINGS

In the rural ministry environment, this can involve surrounding property including the church's cemetery, a field, wooded area, or water from a creek or pond. In the city environment, fast food restaurants, convenience stores, or coffee shops might need to be included in your supervision plan.

As you begin to think through your weekly schedule, it is essential to avoid having unsupervised dead time. It is amazing the ideas that teenagers can develop when they are bored. You will want to consider supervision for the parking lot and outside hang out places when teenagers are gathered. You never know who may drive through your parking lot looking for a student that is wandering around.

BE EXTRA VIGILANT AT SPECIAL EVENTS

Events can be a challenge because the standard protocols may not be in place for supervision, security, and surveillance at your church or at the site to which you are traveling. A lock-in or fifth quarter are great examples of events that need extra measures of supervision and security to protect your people and ministry. The best-organized events can still have students who sneak off or try to push the envelope with their group of friends. Events are usually times we try to get students to bring friends. Many times, we do not know the friends as well as we know the weekly teenagers who are faithful to church. Consider vetted volunteers, with procedures for keeping up with the kids so you do not trip up on your event.

NO ONE NEEDS TO BE ALONE

Students should not be alone during an event or while on property. The supervision or lack of should never reach the threshold of negligence.

GET THE WORD OUT

Published start and end times to events and the weekly schedule can aid in parents knowing when supervision is scheduled. Parents of a licensed teenage driver should be able to confirm their teenager's attendance for youth events and activities. Some teenagers will use the church youth events as a cover to do other things since they are driving themselves and thus the youth ministry needs the means to verify participation. Published details for parents can help avoid the excuse that the student was late getting home because the event ran late. Text messaging has been a youth minister's dream for letting parents know when the bus will arrive back in the parking lot.

Supervision, security, and surveillance can break down, and you need to be able to defend and provide policy documents to prove your due diligence in these areas. Although you should not focus on security just to be defendable in court, it is important to be able to have written documents to prove your steps in protecting the youth at your church. Believe me when I say I want to stay out of court. However, I believe our motivation should go beyond just being defendable, but to shepherd those God has entrusted into our care.

As a ministry of the church, our motivation should be like the shepherd with his sheep that desires to protect them from harm. When we provide proper supervision and security, we are doing all we can to protect the teenagers from harm within the ministry and from outside threats. You may have pushback in casting a vision for stepping up in these areas, but it is an investment that needs to be made. I believe these concerns impact all sizes of youth groups in our churches. The threats are real, and the harm can happen any given Sunday, Wednesday, or at any event. In recent days, catastrophic events happening with people I trusted has caused me to believe this reality even more. Proverbs chapter two focuses on wisdom that provides security:

"For the Lord gives wisdom; from his mouth come knowledge and understanding. He holds success in store for the upright, he is a shield to those whose walk is blameless, for he guards the course of the just and protects the way of his faithful ones. Then you will understand what is right and just and fair—every good path. For wisdom will enter your heart, and knowledge will be pleasant to your soul. Discretion will protect you, and understanding will guard you." (NIV)

Discretion and understanding are two keywords that are important as you deal with the issue of risk management, specifically with supervision, surveillance, and security. The Lord watches over our work, but many churches have found that their discretion lacked the care needed to supervise their youth ministry. Those people, youth ministry, and churches have picked up the tattered pieces and moved forward. Use discretion as you safeguard the ministry entrusted to you.

QUESTIONS TO CONSIDER:

1. How do you secure your youth space from outside threats during your weekly scheduled times as well as your special events?

2. Do you ever assign youth workers to be a perimeter overseer of your group as you meet? How quickly could you pull something like this off?

3. How do you communicate a problem or suspicion without alarming your entire youth group?

4. Do you feel that you are offering a safe and secure youth environment for your ministry? How and why?

CHAPTER TEN: PREPARING PROPER POLICY

BY DR. JODY DEAN

You've no doubt heard the phrase, "It is better to ask for forgiveness than permission." This popular quote has been used and promoted for various justifications for people's actions. In many situations, I can understand this philosophy because leadership structures can be hard to work through in any organization including the church. The rationale is that if it's a good idea, then moving forward is easier than first gaining permission. And yet, we all know that it's usually a mantra we employ when wanting to act on our initiative outside of a structure that would probably be disapproving of our decision.

Just because something is a good idea doesn't mean that we can pursue it. When it comes to youth ministry, having a good policy in place helps to function as the framework for determining the standard best practices. It helps us know which good ideas to act on, and which to let go of.

Rules and policies should only be articulated if they are necessary, but they should exist in the background of every decision made by your ministry. Guidelines as to when a policy or rule is needed should be described, as well as samples of "good" policies. Policies bring an additional level of accountability. Policies include guidelines for forms, transportation, contracts, rental agreements, and other aspects that direct a pathway your ministry should follow.

A mentor of mine once stated, "it is better to have in place an adequate organization and strong operational policies than to try to solve problems as they occur."[21] Many times we take the approach of, "I will wait and deal with that if it ever happens in my ministry." I believe that Scripture teaches us to protect both the people and the ministry we're entrusted with (see Proverbs 15:21-22, Exodus 18, 2 Timothy 2:14-26, Acts 15). Proper policies create a pathway of prevention instead of problem-solving as issues present themselves. Policies can take a great deal of energy to build, but once they are constructed, implemented, and enforced, one cannot be plagued by jumping from one problem to the next.

So how do you go about crafting these policies? The first step would be to discover any policies created for the entire church that deal with facilities, volunteers, and transportation. Evaluate these policies to determine if they are adequate for youth ministry. Then create a student/parent handbook that is youth ministry specific and includes the overall policies that apply, and add the additional components needed.

Schools provide student/parent handbooks as a guideline in communicating what is expected, what the policies are, why they exist, how discipline for inappropriate actions will be handled, and ensures accountability that the handbook has been read and understood. In ministry where accountability is part of our spiritual maturity process, we should have a system in place that allows for an understanding of guidelines and policies by all involved in the ministry. These guidelines and policies should not limit the ministry, but protect all that are involved so the mission can be accomplished. We also need to be sure we have redemptive solutions in our policies for when they are broken.

When policies are created and adopted by the church, they become guidelines that should be legally defendable. You need to follow what you create and need to be sure they are endorsed by the church in accordance with the church bylaws and trustees. A policy should be complimentary of your ministry, covered by your insurance, and defendable in court.

We have already covered many aspects in other chapters that will be part of your policies; however, I want to present considerations for creating policies for youth ministry that would be beneficial to any youth ministry. Here are a few:

ONLY HAVE OPEN-DOOR MEETINGS
When you or any other adult volunteer are counseling or mentoring a teenager, you should strongly consider an open-door policy. Privacy and accountability should be considered by having an observable meeting. This will prevent getting into a situation of your word against someone else's word.

JUST SAY NO TO STUDENT DRIVERS
Students should never drive on behalf of the church. A Disciple Now is an example where high school students like to drive to host homes or for a church event that is local but meets first at the church. If possible, consider having the church provide approved adult drivers to transport teenagers and adults for all events. In addition, adults should have a clean driving record for their personal vehicle if carrying people for the event.

THREE TO A ROOM AT SLEEPOVERS AND HOTELS
Sleeping arrangements can be a challenge in hotel rooms, during a retreat, camp, mission trip, or an event at a home. The best policy is a minimum of three, each person to their own bed, sleeping bag, or cot. Another non-negotiable when traveling overnight is a same-gender policy with no two unrelated people sharing a bed.

GET A DISCIPLINARY ACTION PLAN
Discipline is a hard issue for youth ministry because every family approaches this subject in their own way. However, a policy can be crafted for overarching guidelines that the youth ministry, participants, and guardians need to have an understanding about. This policy should list the degrees of offenses that merit any disciplinary action. An action plan that describes the process for dealing with disciplinary issues and documentation for incidents when they occur is needed. A written policy will eliminate confusion and clarify concerns for conduct that is unbecoming of the youth ministry.

CREATE CHAPERONE EXPECTATIONS
Chaperone policies can be the best way to avoid having adults being involved that like to travel or observe, but do not want to mix it up with teenagers or do the dirty work of serving. Knowing what is expected of an adult volunteer or chaperone helps clear up this potential confusion. Create standards and expectations for chaperones that are outlined in your policy. Another component of this policy should be the selection process for your ministry. It would be wise if this policy is complementary to other leadership qualifications and background checks for volunteers with minors.

BE MONEY-WISE IN YOUR POLICIES
Payments and refunds for ministry activity are a part of the ministry that can cause sudden confusion. When you are dealing with big-ticket items concerning camp or mission trip, some families may desire to pay over the year as a payment plan. A policy outlining payments and designating those funds so they are not spent on other activities is crucial for maintaining the integrity of receiving payments for trips, events, and resources. A refund policy is also needed to explain that once the church has obligated funds based on your commitment to attend or participate, then no refunds can be given.

Honorable stewardship does not allow for the church to waste money once it is committed. In youth ministry, sometimes another teenager may be able to fill the spot, but that is not always the option. A policy explaining the refund rules will help clarify potential trouble spots for families and you as the minister.

DEFINE YOUR VOLUNTEER POLICY
Volunteer policies are essential for any ministry that deals with minors. We addressed the concern for vetting volunteers in a previous chapter. All vetting, chaperoning, teaching, and serving in regards to volunteers should have a clear policy. This includes any component that extends beyond the church and church-sanctioned activities. In youth ministry, an adult volunteer from another church may desire to attend an event or chaperone a trip because their teenager wants to participate. The volunteers for all aspects of your ministry need to follow the same non-negotiable vetting process and be in compliance with all policies at your church for working with minors. A volunteer policy is vital to protecting the young people entrusted to the church.

PAY ATTENTION TO SECURITY

Security has been addressed in a separate chapter but is mentioned again because a well-crafted policy is necessary for protecting your people, facility, and ministry. This policy should extend to travel, special events, and the weekly gatherings at your church.

What are the primary components for policy and procedure? "A policy is a general statement that relates the church's position on a particular subject."[22] A well-written policy should help the church achieve their stated mission and objectives, provide managerial guidelines for decisions, guide routine operations, and be approved by the church. Each policy should also have procedures to follow that advise the church how to follow and implement policy.[23]

QUESTIONS TO CONSIDER:

1. Review your current policy and ask what is followed and what is avoided or neglected.

2. After reviewing your policies, decide what components or policies need to be added for your ministry or church.

3. How do you plan to address vague or ambiguous areas that could be an issue if something were to occur and the policy needed to be enforced?

CHAPTER ELEVEN: KEEPING UP WITH THE KIDS

BY DR. JODY DEAN

Few things strike more fear into the hearts of youth workers than trying to keep track of students.

There's always that one student who manages to create a Home Alone experience when you merely counted heads instead of checking names. Parents don't appreciate it when they learn that you've left their kid in another state. The old youth minister joke that involves leaving a student or two behind at a highway rest stop because they missed the departure time is a serious issue. As the leader, we have to enforce tactics to keep up with all the students entrusted to us.

You may have experienced a middle school dad who shows up after Wednesday night worship to claim his son, but that son is not on site. You think you saw him earlier but cannot account for sure whether the student was ever in the building. The father claims he was present because he dropped his son off in the parking lot, but no one can verify that the student entered and arrived in the youth room in the building. It's not a fun scenario to consider.

It's vital that we have proper procedures for checking in students. A check-in system provides several layers of accountability. First, the system allows, in times of emergency, not only a number but also names for the students present. A form that accompanies the registration provides emergency contact as well as ministry follow-up information if the family is unchurched. Second, a check-in system allows the staff and volunteers accountability if a student were to leave the building after drop off or never arrived at the youth area during your scheduled time. Knowing with certainty whether or not the student is present would prevent the student's word against the adult.

Many churches offer check-in for preschool and children, but in today's society, any ministry to minors would be well served to have a system that provides an accountable record of attendance with information about allergies, contact for guardian, and physical health conditions.

As we think about how we track students, here are a few considerations to ponder:

KNOW YOUR FORMS
What forms are being utilized in your ministry to have the information you need about a family in case of emergency during your weekly schedule? What resources do you have in place if a student were to become missing or ill under your watch? These forms can also reveal any family circumstances that would prevent a family member from picking up a minor for whom they no longer have custody rights. Although many people in our churches are aware of issues in a family, often we are unaware, or our volunteers do not know the safety concerns.

COUNT MORE THAN ONCE
What system does your church have to know how many students are on the trip, attending the event, or on-campus for your scheduled ministry? A parent being in the parking lot when the bus rolls up only to learn that their child was left at the pit stop does not show a ministry that desires to protect. A student that leaves during the event in their own vehicle, gets picked up by a friend, or walks off campus, can lead to a ministry crisis that does not minister to the teenager or family. If your church were to experience a weather warning or catastrophic issue while you are gathered, do you have a check-in system that would account by name who is in attendance?

As you read through, you may think that this is overkill; however, in the changing world where parents' concerns are increasing concerning safety as well as liability, we have to rethink our systems. Headlines continue to appear about catastrophic issues, and your youth ministry needs to have a system for keeping up with kids that is more than a head count. I pray you never have a lock-down situation or threat at your church from an active shooter or another outside threat, but if you do, good check-in systems can be invaluable in times of crisis.

CHECK-IN AND CHECK-OUT
Students who attend youth events at church should sign in somehow. You should have a system that is agreed upon by leadership and explained to guardians, adult leaders, and students. Teenagers may not desire to "check-in" like the preschool or children's areas of your church, but they are familiar with a system. Students in public and private schools are familiar with terms like "checking out early" and "tardy." Besides, in their extracurricular life, they are accustomed to purchasing tickets to events to be admitted. The point is that teenagers are used to being accounted for. (Not that you should charge admission for youth events!) Theaters, sports arenas, and schools take these steps for security, and there's no reason why the church should not follow suit.

THROW OUT THE "BUDDY SYSTEM"
Students who attend a youth trip should be instructed/required to check in at appointed times. The "buddy system" breaks down if both buddies are missing! Many churches do a better job when they are traveling than during their weekly schedule for having a list of participants and periodically checking the list. The weekly scheduled events occurring within the church facility should consider the following options for keeping with up with their students. At least six options currently exist for a secure check-in system.

>1. A biometric scan that reads the fingerprint and verifies the person's identity can be a quick and efficient way for a teenager to record their presence upon arrival.
>
>2. A key tag with a scan bar code that is similar to many business reward programs and the unique bar code is assigned to each family. One caution is that a friend could loan their key tag to a friend for check-in.
>
>3. A plastic card that is the shape of a driver's license or credit card that has the scan bar code on the card.
>
>4. A touchscreen check-in system like utilized by airlines for checking into a flight for a boarding pass.
>
>5. The search system utilizes personal information like the last four digits of a phone number or first four letters of the last name of the family.
>
>6. Mobile apps that allow for check-in through the smart device of the parent. All of these systems then can print labels for identification of the child at church that are given to workers. Then parent/guardian has a label for child pick-up.[24]

The check-in and out procedure vary widely across churches with many having no system at all. The two aspects to consider for protecting your students are ensuring you have an accountable check-in system when you are gathering each week, and a system for adult chaperone accountability for those attending events while in transit, at the event, and during pit-stops.

The responsibility of keeping up with minors resides with the adults, not the teenager or their peers. We do not want to create the encounter Mary and Joseph had with Jesus in the caravan during travel of getting to a location and realizing a middle schooler has disappeared. Although Jesus ended up being back at the building and amazed his parents did not discern where He was (you have seen this conversation between a middle schooler and mom before), the reality is Mary and Joseph thought that since their son was with the group, he could not be lost (Luke 2: 41-52). Creating safeguards in our weekly times of worship, Bible study, and other events help minimize chaos, maintain safeguards, and ultimately create more meaningful ministry environments.

QUESTIONS TO CONSIDER:

1. What ways can teenagers be unaccounted for when you are gathered at the church property?

2. What process do you have for keeping up with students when traveling or at events?

3. What steps do you need to consider to more effectively keep up with the teenagers in your ministry?

CHAPTER TWELVE: UNPACKING THE UNEXPECTED

BY DR. JODY DEAN

We've all been impacted by "the unexpected." When the unexpected strikes, legendary stories result. You may have your own version of the "top five unexpected stories" that are as legendary as your favorite camp t-shirt. Here are mine in no particular order:

1. The unexpected moment when the bus lost its engine on an incline en-route to youth camp (FYI: you cannot get towed with a loaded vehicle). We now had two issues on the side of the interstate: what to do with a bus full of kids and adults, and how to get the bus towed.

2. The unexpected moment when the teenager on the fourth floor sets off the fire sprinkler by accident and floods a four-story building. (I enjoy telling this one because relocating a whole group in the middle of the night in Gatlinburg in February just makes you want to minister to teenagers for life.)

3. The unexpected moment when two chaperones are arguing so fiercely at midnight that they begin tossing luggage off the second-floor balcony. (Makes for some great camp memories.)

4. The unexpected moment during an icebreaker where a student, who has been tied up like a mummy, falls through the sheetrock wall. It was a sad day to be sheetrock! (Also, this may have happened twice in two different churches.)

5. The unexpected moment when, upon arriving at camp, getting stung by a wasp on the way to registration. Benadryl is helpful for the wasp sting, but not for being an alert caretaker to students. (Then while registering, a maintenance guy comes in to report he backed into a parked vehicle in the parking lot. You guessed it: my vehicle!)

Youth ministers need a plan for the "unexpected," even as by nature they are difficult to plan for. There is an excellent example from Scripture. We can imagine the Apostle Paul teaching into the evening and the young man Eutychus listening intently at first. But as time wears on, Eutychus begins to nod and then falls into a deep sleep. He falls three stories to his death, and Paul goes down and brings him back to life. Recorded in Acts 20, this story reveals a truth today. In ministry, the unexpected can occur. Paul provided an example through this fatal accident of how to be level-headed in our responses to the unexpected and minister through crises. While we may not have the ability to always perform miracles, we can be mindful of the unexpected challenges youth ministry creates.

But it's not just students. I have taken more adults to the ER than students over the years. Before departure on a trip, you have to consider who can be in charge if you have to leave the group to care for someone in an emergency. The shepherding process is crucial at this point. If you are an adult in youth ministry, you will eventually experience the unexpected: a medical emergency, illegal activity, or someone causing harm to the ministry from the outside. I remember a camp week with two ER trips for two different teenagers, a youth who brought illegal substances, and an active shooter threat to an outdoor event on church property. Hopefully, you do not experience these emergencies, but you need to have a plan that adults can execute to protect those involved in your ministry.

Another consideration for the unexpected is severe weather. Different types of severe weather (whether a hurricane, tornado, earthquake, snow, wildfire and so on) require you to have a weather policy for your ministry that mirrors the protocols of a public school system. You are not always warned or prepared for these unexpected events. A tornado warning during youth group is a scary event and being a leader that can stay calm in these events and be there for your teenagers is important.

As we consider what it looks like to lead through these unexpected events, here are some prompts for your thoughts:

FIND THE HELPERS
Nurses, doctors, and paramedics in your church can be a great resource when you are dealing with unexpected through medical issues. These people can be a front line to deal with the injured, while others deal with the entire group and adults are deployed to secure the area and direct the medical personnel when upon arrival.

Don't forget that food allergies can be a serious concern. A kid that begins to feel sick can become very ill in no time. Recently I was chaperoning a trip where a child went from playing and participating in outdoor recreation to being between two hospitals and admitted to ICU within less than six hours. Any sickness or reaction should be treated with serious attention because you are (most likely) not a doctor. It's not possible for you as a youth minister to diagnose the severity of a student's illness.

KEEP A RECORD
Legal considerations should be factored as you deal with accidents, medical emergencies, facility or equipment malfunctions, and weather procedures. Most ministers and volunteers do not consider writing down the details during the unexpected,

but a report of the incident is a needed artifact. These situations can become a legal matter very quickly, and being prepared to answer the questions can be a crucial consideration in dealing with the unexpected. My chaperone list, student list, packing list, rental agreement and any media taken during the event have been questioned when unpacking the unexpected.

REMEMBER YOUR ROLE
You need to minister to the individual who is injured, but do not forget to lead and minister to the group as a whole during the unexpected. You need clear discernment for the student who never feels well and always needs attention. In the one time you ignore the student, it could actually be a tragic, unexpected medical issue. You should treat every concern as serious until you know differently.

MAKE FRIENDS IN LAW ENFORCEMENT
Make it a priority to know police and authority contacts and be as prepared as possible when the unexpected occurs. Keep these contacts on speed dial so you can immediately reach out to them when an emergency or crisis event occurs. Whether it's a domestic issue in a family, an accidental fire alarm pull, or off the record advice, an established relationship with local authorities can prove to be beneficial in navigating unexpected circumstances.

KEEP INFORMATION READILY AVAILABLE
What information do you need each week during regularly scheduled ministry and for each trip concerning every teenager and volunteer involved? Many times, we will have a medical release form for a trip, but what about during your regularly scheduled weekly events? You should have a file of emergency information to treat the student and contact the guardian. (This can also aid in preventing the unauthorized parent that does not have custody from arriving and picking up their child.)

HAVE A TRANSPORTATION SAFETY PLAN BEFORE YOU NEED IT
If you don't have a bus breakdown or a 15-passenger van tire blow-out while traveling for camp, then you are fortunate. When a vehicle breaks down, your number one priority should be the safety of the passengers. They need to be away from traffic and out of danger. Think through your safety plan when the unexpected break down occurs. You may need to pack a breakdown kit with water, snacks, and necessary items from flashlights to reflective vests. Transportation issues can be frustrating and stressful from the delay on the road to the exhaustion of dealing with the vehicle and the students. You need to think through these situations so you can keep your own emotions in check and minister to your group. Adult volunteers are crucial during a breakdown and can be vital in keeping a positive group attitude.

DESIGNATE A BACK-UP
Accidents occur on the best and worst of days in ministry. From a kid slamming a door on a teacher's hand or a fall going up the steps, to two guys colliding in a

head-on-collision during a game, these are just some examples of unexpected outcomes. Having an adult volunteer or co-minister who you trust to take over will free you up to go with people to the hospital or relay information to parents.

BE WEATHER-WISE
A weather warning is nothing to sneeze at when planning your ministry and events. High school athletics have outdoor lightning delays for a reason. If you have an outdoor sports league, game on Wednesday night, or special event, then you should consider weather warnings and have a policy for lightning and other severe weather. You may deal with hurricanes, tornadoes, snow, or ice based on your geographical location. Most people live in a place where they deal with some form of severe weather, and you need to plan for the unexpected weather event.

TAKE EVEN THE SMALL THINGS INTO CONSIDERATION
Power outages and other mechanical issues in your building or when traveling can create unique ministry moments. The air conditioning or heat malfunctioning can cause a retreat to be miserable or in extreme cases canceled. When the power outage occurs, you learn quickly how few windows were installed in your building during construction. A lack of lighting or extreme temperatures are unexpected variables that must be considered for the safety of your people. Tile flooring can begin to sweat when the power fails, and a lack of climate control can cause a dangerous situation with a high risk of injury.

I have visited the ER with youth and adults in town and during various mission trips and camps. The power has gone out during a youth rally involving several churches that caused a unique worship experience. Various buses and vans have left me stranded and struggling to transport a group of people during a trip. A stomach virus outbreak on a retreat may have been the worst unexpected event during my ministry. These are just a few of my crazy experiences of the unexpected. You will encounter your own. So be prepared to lead well and minister to your people as the unexpected occurs.

QUESTIONS TO CONSIDER:

1. Do you have a list of medically trained people in your church that can help during a medical emergency? If not, what is your plan to build that list as soon as possible?

2. What policy and protocols do you have in place for a transportation break down?

3. Do you maintain records for your ministry volunteers and participants each week or just trips? Create a form and plan for keeping current information for the people in your ministry.

4. Do you have a severe weather plan and policy in place for your church and facility? If not, who can you call that might? There's no need to recreate one when a friend may have one on file.

PART 4

SHEPHERDING THE ENVIRONMENT AND CULTURE

The final section in the book is highly pragmatic—any one of you could have written it as it comes out of personal experience more than from case law, insurance regulations, or the threat of litigation or accusation. The first chapter asks that you take a critical tour around your church facility. Are there issues with broken sidewalks, unsecured playground equipment, or faulty wiring? ***Tripping up on Trips*** is a discussion of the obvious—when you leave the environment of the church that you have structured for safety, an extra layer of preparation is necessary. Bad things can happen on buses and vans and in hotels and retreat facilities.

Negating Negligence is a restatement of the obvious—all the risk management in the world is in vain if a youth pastor, another staff member, volunteer or intern is guilty of negligence. If policies and procedures are ignored and negligent supervision puts people or property in harm's way, then all bets are off.

The final chapter on contemporary issues is a catch-all. Acknowledging that we cannot be exhaustive, we attempted to discuss some of the recent topics that have made the news cycle (issues such as gender inclusion, ministering to LGBTQ+ students, social media concerns, etc.) that have created interesting conversations for churches.

CHAPTER THIRTEEN: FACING FAULTY FACILITIES

BY DR. JODY DEAN

Jack Crabtree wrote the flagship book on risk management in youth ministry, *Better Safe than Sued*. Crabtree identified a category of potential danger he called "safety sins," and reminded youth ministers about being on the lookout for unsafe conditions in and around the church. We tend to see some things so often that we don't see them at all, things like broken concrete on a walkway or a missing handrail on a stairway.

I still remember the clumsy kid tripping and falling through the wall. The silhouette of a middle school student hollowed out of a wall can be hard to explain, but most adults in our ministries understand accidents. This chapter intends to unpack the closets, dark corners, parking lots, and other places that could become a faulty link in the chain. We get accustomed to our space because we are in it week in and week out. However, we need to develop a sense of awareness of dangers that could be lurking through our facilities.

Let's begin a virtual walk around of your space. These considerations will help you identify faulty facility components and help you create a checklist for future check-ups.

1. Does the perimeter of the property outside have working perimeter lighting, parking lot lights that are on when dark, and entrances that are well lit?

2. Does your church have indoor directional signage that clearly directs people and guests to the locations for your weekly small groups, activities, and special events? A great way to test this is to have a friend from another church try to navigate your building.

3. How clean is your space? Clean is an achievable standard in any size ministry. You should be sure the trash, restrooms, stairwells, and hallways are clear and clean. The clutter under stairwells and closets should be organized, labeled, and removed if against fire code.

Many youth ministries have received a reputation for trashing vehicles and spaces after events. If your church has a cleaning and maintenance staff, be respectful of their time. If your special event on the weekend is after your cleaning staff has completed their preparation for Sunday, create a plan with volunteers to be sure the facility is ready for worship.

4. Is your space age-appropriate? Teenagers do not want to be considered children, but yet they will play on a playground or ride a tricycle trying to be funny. Is the space designated for youth set up to allow for community and accomplishing the goals you've set for your ministry? You may not have the ideal room or area for your group. Coffee shops have embraced the multi-use concept from a friendly group of chairs that allows for more private chatting, a group of tables for study and conversation, or a long table designed for a group of people to gather.

Perhaps your church does not have a dedicated youth space. You might have a shared space that must consider all the ministries and people who utilize that particular square footage. Also, consider how the gym, kitchen, and fellowship areas can be cleaner and more organized than when you arrived. You can set the standard for clean facilities that are inviting.

5. Is your space accessible to all students? Accessibility for those with disabilities may not be a requirement for every part of your facility, but you need to keep in mind the needs of a person with disabilities who desires to attend. Even if you do not currently have a student that needs accommodation, there will be times when an injured student might need these types of considerations for a season. Your facilities must include access to Bible study, events, restrooms, worship, and other places a teenager may need to traverse your building when you gather.

6. How are you dealing with bathrooms? Bathrooms and supervision have become a point of consideration due to the changing culture. We will not deal in this section with the transgender issue, but you do need to be aware that as teenagers come, the issues facing teenagers also arrive with them.

We rarely think that it's a safety issue when a minor leaves unaccompanied to use the restroom at another location within your facility. But maybe we should. Teenagers can wander and find themselves in places in your facility that you did not intend. (An example is a teenager who needs to go to the restroom, but decides to go to her mom's preschool classroom when finished. Then the issue becomes whether she is authorized to serve around preschoolers.) The youth area has the responsibility to protect others within the facilities. Any participant in your ministry needs to stay in authorized areas doing what they are scheduled to be doing, and you are in charge of those boundaries.

7. Are you maintaining visibility? Classrooms with windows have become an increasing standard for many churches. I encourage windows in each classroom and office

for accountability. These windows should not be obscured with curtains and decorations to allow for visibility from the hallways. You may even find it beneficial for closets also to have a window.

8. Is there an opportunity to be alone? Do not let dark corners or prayer rooms become the make-out room. Walk the facility and ensure that proper supervision is occurring in all areas of the church where students might find some alone time. Sometimes we forget that teenagers will push parameters as they are going through a season of discovery. If your church facility provides opportunities, then do not be surprised if someone uses that opportunity.

9. Have you cleared the walkways? The propped-up table or props along hallways or on the stage can cause harm to the teenager that bumps into them. A broken toe, scraped leg, or broken limb can be an issue if items were not stored properly.

10. Do you need to lock down unused spaces? Many of us remember playing fun games in a dark, empty church after Wednesday night youth group. A dark facility with places to hide does not present the safest venue for running or navigating, which can result in injury. You need to be sure the rooms that can cause harm with equipment or people are locked during occupied hours. Consider the entire youth group and your facility when planning your events. Liability advice for facilities can be found through resources from your insurance provider.

11. Is there a solution for storage? Storing supplies can be hazardous or disastrous if done improperly or left for curious scientists to experiment. You should date and label supplies from food, chemicals, paint, and outdoor equipment that has expiration dates. You may regret it if you are tired after Wednesday night and just shove items into a closet or dump all the retreat stuff in your storage area to be sorted later. Take the time to put things away correctly. Explaining why the youth supply closet started the fire that burned down the church may not be the resume builder you are looking for.

12. Do you have a gym? Gyms can be a blessing and a curse because you enjoy the space, but you may not have the policies that govern its usage. Youth ministry must consider the entire church and community when utilizing the gym. Many youth ministries get contacted by outside organizations that desire to use the space. Have contractual agreements with agreed upon guidelines for facility use when people desire to use your facility. Consider how to handle injuries from sprains, concussions, or worse, before your first injury. Also, consider a plan for supervision for everyone's safety.

13. Are you on the same team as the rest of your staff? The building superintendent, custodial staff, and properties committee should not despise youth ministry because they always are dealing with broken things or problems. We know that dealing with teenagers will require the occasional touch-up paint, broken light, or unexplainable "not-sure-how-that-happened"

Monday morning. Build relationships with these people, and help them understand the bigger picture of making disciples of teenagers and their families. Also, used space is a good thing, but be sure that your ministry also understands the difference between worn and mistreated. Accidents happen even within the best guidelines, so your facility should stay ahead of maintenance to remain well maintained and not just worn out.

QUESTIONS TO CONSIDER:

1. Take a tour as if you are a first-time guest from arriving on property, getting inside, and navigating where to go. What did you learn from your tour of your space?

2. What considerations are you doing well with your facilities?

3. What parts of your facility need attention and improvement?

4. What organizational structure do you need to work with to address your concerns?

CHAPTER FOURTEEN: TRIPPING UP ON TRIPS

BY DR. JODY DEAN

In 2018, every news outlet had a headline about a soccer team and their coach who were trapped in a cave due to unexpected rising water in Thailand. It was a riveting story that captivated the world. What was a simple walk into a cave turned into a life and death ordeal.

Simple excursions have the potential to trip up our best intentions. The rescue of the soccer team and the bravery of their young coach are extraordinary. The loss of life of one rescuer is also tragic. As we plan for trips in our ministries, the potential to miscalculate requires us to plan and organize well before we even depart for a trip.

It used to be so simple: "Everybody get in the van! We are going to the water park." In contemporary culture, good common sense has rightfully replaced some of the recklessness of days gone by. Yet a risk assessment is needed to determine if youth ministry should embrace risks such as bungee-jumping, rock or mountain climbing, and mechanical bull riding just to name a few (or anything mentioned in a country song). You have to weigh the risks of activities that could harm your ability to accomplish the vision and mission of your ministry and church.

Transportation, chaperones, and guidelines for your travel are vital components to a trip. When people go on vacation, they usually escape from their normal routine and will be adventurous, try different foods, and seek daring activities. The rules (think bedtimes and routines) are different on family vacation. This mindset can extend to youth ministry trips, and thus more trouble or increased risk can occur than regularly exists in your weekly ministry to teens.

As a leader, you need to cast a vision for your trips. Provide detailed information and policies so people do not trip up, hijacking the intent of the trip's purpose. Very few trips occur without an episode of the unexpected. A stomach virus, a flat tire on the bus, or an accidental injury are almost givens when traveling because it seems something always happens. Let's consider a few items that will help you to avoid tripping up on trips.

PREPARATION IS KEY
Being prepared for travel is the obvious answer for not tripping up during a trip. The details can be a challenge. Directions, forms, items to bring, ministry packing list, transportation needs, training and equipping chaperones, and communicating with participants and their guardians is a long list of administrative details that many choose to ignore. The preparation should move beyond administrative detail to focus on the spiritual preparation needed for a trip. Jesus modeled being spiritually prepared for trips with the disciples.

KNOW YOUR DOCUMENTS
Each trip requires certain documents. You should have all essential documents copied and copies given to a trusted chaperone, the church office, and yourself. It's okay to keep a copy of these on our phones, but don't place your trust in wi-fi or a full battery. The essential documents should include a notarized medical release form for each participant (teenager and adult), any documents or agreements needed for the ministry or retreat center from participants, and copies of the contracts or agreements for any organization whose services are being utilized during the trip.

DOUBLE UP ON KEYS
Have two sets of keys for vehicles. You never know when they will get lost or locked inside the vehicle.

RESERVE FACILITIES AND RETREAT CENTERS THAT MEET THE NEEDS OF THE GROUP
Sometimes we will use a place we have outgrown because we like the setting for our event; however, if it does not meet the needs of your group, it is a bad start to your trip.

One of the biggest mistakes I have ever made in youth ministry is using a retreat center that did not meet the needs of my teenagers. Whining grows old, and emotions soar when accommodations are not ideal. And it is incredible how adults can sometimes be the negative force that causes the teenagers to view the retreat and facilities differently due to the demeanor of the chaperones.

INVESTIGATE PROPER AUTHORIZATIONS
Having the proper authorizations from parents and guardians may seem logical, but airports and retreat centers will reject minors without proper guardian authorization for travel or participation. A best practice would be for you to investigate the requirements for the providers or services you are utilizing and what they require for each participant. Also, be sure the trustees of your organization have approved and signed the agreements for contracts during your trip.

DESIGNATE A MEDICAL CHAPERONE
Take care of medications for students and do not allow teenagers to manage their

medicines. You do not want anyone sharing, and medicine should be taken as scheduled. Food allergies are another crucial aspect that must be taken seriously. If certain medications or an epi-pen may be needed, then be sure you and a volunteer can administer those in a critical moment.

Before your trip, scout the closest walk-in clinic and hospitals, because you never know when one will be needed. Don't rely too heavily on your smartphone. Some trips place us more off-grid with limited service. Have a binder with all critical information already printed and available. Help guardians understand that medicines need to continue during the trip. Most parents will know this, but you do not want to get into a situation where attention deficit or emotional medications are not sent on a trip, and a teenager experiences trauma due to detox.

You will need a release from a guardian to administer the medications as prescribed. Part of the medical chaperone's responsibilities should be first aid administration. I like to travel with a stocked backpack of supplies for the basics to covers scrapes, burns, stings, and headaches. Take all medical concerns seriously, as activity for a teenager can be altered during a trip. They can be more active than usual, change their eating patterns, or be hiding an issue that is masked during the week but is exposed on a trip. Educate yourself on your students and walk carefully through the medical issues that can occur during a trip. Special event medical insurance may be an item you purchase for each participant on each trip to cover the unexpected.

COME BACK WITH THE SAME PEOPLE YOU LEFT WITH

Assigning teenagers to adults was covered briefly during the weekly suggestions for keeping up with the kids. It is important that during a trip, the adults have assigned teenagers they are keeping track of. Do not rely on just a buddy system for rest stops and restaurants. Initiate a roll call of names that does not just depend on head counts. Returning with the same people that departed on the trip is an important step to avoid tripping up.

PLAN FOR PIT STOPS AND MEALS AS YOU TRAVEL

Help restaurants and retail spaces out. I would call ahead of a meal stop when traveling and warn the fast food place of the coming onslaught. The places would be better prepared for a line of constant orders, and as a result, the stops were quicker with more efficient service.

Limit your stops as much as possible. If you are the trip planner that stops whenever you feel like it and have a group of people that function with that philosophy, you will struggle to keep up with people. Packing snacks purchased in bulk can save families money. If you manage snacks for the group, the spending money budget can be maintained. Unfortunately, I have never traveled without someone running low on their funds for various reasons. I always traveled with extra and offered my chaperones reimbursement if they overspent their budget helping students in need.

HAVE A CONFLICT MANAGEMENT PLAN IN PLACE

Communicate a plan for conflict, the process for being sent home, or consequences for breaking rules that do not result in being sent home. When people become enraged with each other over words, actions, or events, it is essential to be able with chaperones to cool the situation and remove the teenagers from the rest of the group observing. (I believe we should follow the example in Matthew 18 for resolving conflict among teenagers by bringing them to a place of reconciliation with each other.)

The process for being sent home can be beyond your control if the teenager or teenagers break rules of the facility or organization and they request the immediate dismissal. You then must secure a transportation method to return the teenager to their guardian. You will need to think through the party responsible for paying for the unexpected return trip home. Parents should be responsible, but sometimes they cannot afford the expense or expect the church to pay this expense. This is why communicating the rules and consequences before a trip is important. Also, some rules that are broken can be dealt with once the trip is over.

A discipline (not punishment) plan should be in place to help the teenager become a better person and learn from their mistakes. These can become great opportunities for spiritual growth in the teenager's life. Besides, prevention of drugs, alcohol, and violence is best done preemptively and not reactively.

Permission slips, medical release forms, rooming assignments and (unfortunately) procedures to send a student home from a trip are necessary ingredients in youth ministry. Social media has allowed the trip's ups and downs to be communicated immediately to a broader audience. Many times, the funny stories, drama, pictures, God moments, and unfortunate issues can be posted and then await you to unpack as soon as you put the van in park back home.

QUESTIONS TO CONSIDER:

1. Where are areas that you could be tripping up on trips?

2. What key steps can you take to reduce the potential mishaps when traveling?

3. Do you have a travel checklist for your trips? If not, when is a good time for you to get started on one? Put a reminder on your calendar to get started ahead of your next trip.

4. What forms do you need to create for when you travel?

CHAPTER FIFTEEN: NEGATING NEGLIGENCE

BY DR. JODY DEAN

All the risk management strategies in the world cannot combat negligence. Negligence can be a result of carelessness, lack of preparation, or stupidity. Educating volunteers and paid staff on conditions that are ripe for negligence is essential.

Billboards for personal injury lawyers remind us of the liability we all have each day. Every business has liability as they conduct their work, and the church also has liability as we seek to accomplish the work God has called us to lead. The depth of negligence and liability ministers should consider is outlined but not exhaustive as each municipality, state, and country has specific laws for these issues.

Today's culture allows for a lawsuit for any aspect of ministry whether guilty, negligent, or innocent. Many church members still have the mentality that a church or themselves would never or could never be sued as a result of ministry. Trustees, ministers, and ministry volunteers must consider the negligence aspect to their decisions. Gross negligence can result in punitive damages, loss of limited immunity under state law, and personal liability.[25] The ministerial staff lives with the reality of these three aspects of negligence week in and week out. Although the Volunteer Protection Act prohibits many aspects of liability while volunteering, it does not remove all negligence from a volunteer within an organization. A volunteer that conducts "willful or criminal misconduct, gross negligence, reckless misconduct, or a conscious, flagrant indifference to the rights or safety of the individual harmed by the volunteer" is one of four provisions to the Volunteer Protection Act.[26]

The idea of being negligent as a church, minister, or volunteer is far from many Christian's thoughts as they prepare to worship with their congregation week-in and week-out. In the excitement of a trip, a volunteer may forget to check for seatbelts, but after an accident, the answer to this question may determine negligent behavior. Did the church approve a plan or policy for minor's safety during the weekly programs? If the church approved plans and policies and a court can prove that they were not adhered to, then negligence can be affirmed after an incident occurs.

Personal liability is a burden for the minister and youth volunteer during special events and weekly Bible study. The phrase "you can be sued for anything" applies to youth ministry whether for weekend retreats, white water rafting, camp, an after-church cookout at a member's residence, or Wednesday night youth. I could share many examples over several decades of ministry of specific experiences where a parent was understanding, or an event was not considered at the time an issue of negligence on the leader. Today ministerial trust has eroded to where parents are more questioning of the safety, transportation, reputation of a volunteer, or purpose for an event. If trust is an issue or an occurrence questionable, then negligence on the pathways mentioned above are pursuable and valid. The church, minister, and volunteers have to make a concerted effort that shows due diligence to protect the people. This is the best practice to reduce the threat of negligence in your ministry. However, if the properties committee fails to make advised improvements to facilities, transportation is not well maintained with records, volunteers not vetted, or youth concerns not addressed, then the level of negligence and liability increases accordingly with proven allegations. Defendable policy and proven practice can diminish these concerns if they are always in place as you minister. The worst scenario is to loosely follow policy with haphazard practice. This provides evidence that a pattern of negligence was in place.

Negating negligence is hard to overcome if you do not have a valid defense for denying the charge. The personal injury aspect of law brings to light the reality of trying to refute a claim of negligence based on a facility issue, a personnel matter, transportation, or incidents between peers. People's ideas and concepts can be hard to refute when a minor is involved. Youth ministry adults must consider the needed components to negate negligence.

Paperwork for accidents, notarized permission forms, and vetted volunteers are necessary components that should be standard. When you consider a public school and their forms and procedures for dealing with minors, then you begin to understand the level of negligence that can occur when active teenagers are involved. The church is no longer viewed with the forgiving nature when dealing with liability from church members or those attending when a minister, volunteer, or the execution of the event is deemed negligent.

Here are some points to consider:

LOOK THROUGH THE LENS OF NEGLIGENCE
Leaders should scrutinize their weekly ministry offerings, special events, and trips through the lens of negligence. Facilities, training, documentation, and transportation will be suspect when an injury, behavior, or another component of harm occurs. The previous chapters and the considerations presented can aid in reviewing these factors, but negligence is always a possibility when an organization provides a service to minors. You cannot prevent everything, but you can provide a snapshot that you did due diligence in trying to prevent any harm from occurring.

Consider who is responsible for executing contracts on behalf of your organization. A minister or volunteer should defer to a trustee of the organization. This is the best practice for renting facilities or vehicles for a trip, as well as equipment, phones, sanitation, or food for your ministry. Another component to consider: who can sign the agreement or contract on behalf of the church? If you are not authorized to sign, you may be considered liable as a person, without the legal protection of the church. The person might be negligent and liable if they did not have authority from the church to execute contracts or be an authorized signature for the organization. Many churches in their by-laws assign the signature and contract responsibility to trustees.

EDUCATE YOUR VOLUNTEERS
Chaperones and volunteers should understand negligence and how their actions could be considered negligent if they do not adhere to the policies and guidelines of the church and youth ministry. (Examples include a host home that allows for activities that could be questionable during a weekend retreat, or chaperones that allow their teenager and her friends to do something beyond the youth ministry guidelines during a trip.) Adults who spend more time in conversation with each other than chaperoning and being aware of the crowd dynamic could be deemed negligent. A youth minister that tries to be a teenager more than a leader could be considered negligent.

BE AWARE OF WHAT IS AROUND YOU
Facilities, transportation, and outdoor recreation space can cause concern with negligence. If you have aspects to your building that have been neglected or repairs that have been postponed, if something occurred, a negligence claim could be made by the affected party. Transportation is always a risk if drivers are not screened, operate a vehicle in dangerous ways, or maintenance is not completed as scheduled. Playgrounds, ball fields, adjacent property, or vacant land owned by the church carry specific aspects of concern regarding negligence. Each of these considerations should be regularly inspected for maintenance for issues that could present a hazard for those that use them. Posted signs with guidelines should be considered to alert to "play-at-your-own-risk" locations or outline where church property ends.

PAY ATTENTION TO SPECIAL EVENTS
Special events with organizations not affiliated with your church (but being hosted by your church) can cause you to be part of a negligent claim. These claims will then be rejected or assigned partial percentage of negligence based on rental agreements and the nature of your church's relationship with the organization. You also need to consider staff representatives that are present for these events that will represent the church's interest.

KNOW YOUR OWN PROTECTIONS
Review your personal insurance policies to see what protections you have for any accusations of negligence through your residence, vehicle, or for your family as you minister at your church. Many churches have protection for ministers and volun-

teers through the church's insurance coverage. You may want to consider additional personal coverage if you are not sure you are protected from a potential issue. An additional umbrella policy that provides additional legal and financial coverage can be an inexpensive blessing. In ministry I do not want you to worry about serving or sharing your resources within your church and community; however, liability is something we have to consider.

QUESTIONS TO CONSIDER:

1. What rules do you have in place regarding trustees and who is responsible for entering into contracts?

2. What are the responsibilities that you require of volunteers and chaperones? Do you have these written? How do you communicate them to volunteers and chaperones?

3. What policies and guidelines do you have for the use of indoor and outdoor facilities for church-related and non-church related events?

4. If an event occurred with an injury or issue with your people this month, what would your liability exposure as a church, minister, or volunteer be? If you can't answer that questions, it may be time to do a little research.

CHAPTER SIXTEEN: CONSIDERING CONTEMPORARY ISSUES

BY DR. ALLEN JACKSON

I have a confession to make. I don't really know what "contemporary issues" means except that my ministry assignment has changed. For twenty-two years, I taught youth and collegiate ministry at the New Orleans Baptist Theological Seminary. I often spoke on Risk Management. Early in my teaching career, I simply called it "Legal Issues" in youth ministry, and the basic thesis for my lecture was "don't do stupid stuff." Of primary interest were "Safety Sins,"[27] volunteer worker screening, rules of engagement for counseling teenagers, and sound policies for at-church supervision and safeguarding from chaos on trips, topics covered in this book as well.

The concerns of risk management in ministry in general and youth ministry, in particular, were relevant then and are relevant now. They are the reason Dr. Dean and I wanted to write a book that was readable and accessible to youth ministry folks. However, in the year I have been away from the classroom, the impact of the Oberkfell vs. Hodges[28] has shaped the same-sex marriage discussion, and the United States Department of Education issued a directive on gender-neutral bathrooms[29] and various states enacted laws either requiring or forbidding gender-neutral bathrooms. In summer 2015, the Boy Scouts of America, with troops hosted by many churches, changed a policy to allow openly homosexual leaders to guide local troops. A lot has happened in a short time.

In my youth ministry class, "Risk Management" became a three-lecture unit, and later a Doctor of Ministry Seminar. The capstone assignment was a "Risk Management Manual" which was supposed to be a boots-on-the-ground look at what needs to happen in a local church. One assignment in the D.Min Seminar was to enlist a team of persons at the church who might help with a risk management assessment. Ideally, including an insurance person, a law enforcement person, a lawyer, a counselor, and some parents, the team would help the church safeguard property, people, and policies.

Now I am a pastor of a church in the Atlanta, GA area and the while the "legal issues" category is still useful, the scope of what I have faced or heard about already is beyond what I taught. Do churches have a legal obligation to comply with the American Disabilities Act? Do churches have to designate a bathroom as gender neutral? What additional provisions need to be made for special needs students? Will clergy be forced to perform same-sex marriage? It seems like a lot is coming at us in a hurry. A book of this limited scope cannot even address these evolving issues with any authority, but fortunately, there are organizations like the Church Law and Tax Report as well as denominational agencies or other non-profit legal counsel.

The establishment of a risk management team is still a good idea–I have enlisted one here at my church. But the inclusion of a few more specialists may be necessary. The "contemporary issues" category is inclusive of some of the things that have come up in the last two years and represent a new horizon in risk management.

Since it is impossible to give ironclad strategies to issues that are still being unpacked in courtrooms and statehouses, I will just identify a few of them and suggest the challenges ahead.

Considerations:
DEVELOP AND MAINTAIN SOLID ACCOUNTING PRACTICES
With more money and more requirements for churches and other non-profits, it is more important than ever to keep good records, prepare regular reports, and use established accounting practices to keep up with resources provided by both the offerings of church members and the registration money paid by activity attendees.

WHAT IS YOUR SOCIAL MEDIA POLICY?
While Online Obnoxiousness got a chapter of its own, the ongoing innovation in social media with sharing of pictures, personal information, and real-time stream of consciousness thinking (even inappropriate text messages), have created challenges for churches. Does your church have a social media policy reminding staff and lay leaders that their online presence also represents the church they serve?

DIMINISH CRIMES OF OPPORTUNITY
More churches have been victimized by persons who figured out the relatively constant rhythm of the congregation. Sunday morning is an excellent time for a thief to go through the parking lot to find unlocked cars or through unlocked doors into offices or choir rooms where valuables are left behind.

MONITOR CASUAL TRAFFIC
Similar to crimes of opportunity, most churches do not have secure parking lot access. Many churches have open campus designs, allowing vehicle and pedestrian traffic to be unobserved. This is a potentially harmful scenario during a weekday when the preschool or Mother's Day Out is meeting, but security measures are not in place.

ESTABLISH AN ACTIVE SHOOTER PLAN
More churches than you think have had to initiate an active shooter plan. Sometimes urban or suburban churches on busy streets are susceptible to shooting not intended to be directed at them. It is always a possibility that a shooter (disgruntled ex-spouse, someone who doesn't like a stance the church has taken, a mentally-unbalanced person trying to make a statement) invades church space. Local police departments are increasingly helping churches to develop an active shooter plan, and resources are available through ready.gov/active-shooter.

PRACTICE MEDICAL EMERGENCY AND FIRE DRILLS
Pastors and youth pastors who have been serving for a while have experienced a medical emergency when a student got hurt at an activity, or a senior adult volunteer had a heart attack at the church. While this got a chapter of its own (Unpacking the Unexpected), the contemporary task of the church is to make sure that persons know how to tell a first responder to go directly to the scene of the crisis. To say, "come to the fellowship hall" means nothing to an ambulance driver unless they are a member of the church. Fire drills are common in school, but I cannot ever remember one being conducted at church.

PROTECT CYBER RESOURCES
The combination of more information online and churches having fewer resources to dedicate to computers and computer maintenance, a consultation with a cyber-security firm might be a good idea. Any private information, whether financial, personal, or pictorial, must be secured with firewalls from intrusion or virus.

GO DEEP ON BACKGROUND CHECKS
An earlier chapter talked about vetting volunteers, but what about the person who drives the bus or runs the soundboard? What about deacons or host home parents? These people are not volunteers who have a direct teaching assignment with minors but are nonetheless in close proximity to them.

PAY ATTENTION TO ACCESSIBILITY
While churches are not generally legally bound by the American Disabilities Act, a moral and spiritual obligation exists to provide access as possible through hearing augmentation, ramps and elevators, automated doors, and cooperative scheduling.

WHO IS PERMITTED TO PICK UP A CHILD?
Increasingly we must ensure that the "right" parent gives permission or picks up a minor. While encouraging trends are emerging in co-parenting in divorce situations, the possibility remains for a non-custodial parent to use the church as a place to unlawfully pick up a student. Also key is awareness of special situations with foster care. (For example, are foster children allowed to leave the state on a trip?)

THE QUESTION OF LGBTQ+ STUDENTS
All students deserve a safe place to work out their faith. While many churches

would not endorse or condone alternative lifestyles (and both authors would embrace that viewpoint), there is no biblical support to reject someone who is seeking God. Speaking the truth in love is more important than ever.

DEALING WITH MEDIA

Churches should outline a procedure to respond to an accusation or pending litigation. Have discussions now and not when a situation arises regarding response to a false accusation, press releases, and who will be the official spokesperson for the church in the event of impropriety.

INTELLECTUAL PROPERTY AND COPYRIGHT ISSUES

We should take a high ethical stance on proper licensing for lyrics, videos, and images that we use in worship, in publications, and on our websites.

PREPARE FOR THE UNFORTUNATE POSSIBILITY OF CRIMINAL MISBEHAVIOR

As painful as it might be if an accused person is a staff member or a key leader, we need to assume the victim is telling the truth. To err on the side of the accused is to further victimize an already-traumatized student, child, or volunteer.

CONCLUSION

In the end, maybe you were hoping for a one-stop strategy to address it all or maybe a "Psych! Just kidding!" on some the darker issues we can face in ministry. The issues are not easy to deal with, and our writing does not address everything. Nor can we bring full clarity to a specific strategy for you to adopt and follow. What we have provided is a simple read to help you and your people begin a conversation of what to address.

Hopefully, in these pages, you've received some advice to start down the pathway of shepherding your people through the risky concerns when your ministry involves minors. We love teenagers, parents, youth ministry, youth volunteers, and the church. It breaks our heart that many aspects of this book even have to be addressed. We hope that you begin to pray about the concerns, vulnerable areas of your ministry, and the people that can help create a stronger shepherding culture in your church with minors.

Character should be a non-negotiable that leads you to vet your volunteers and safeguard all areas of your ministry, even the finances. The people we minister to will have concerns or issues that need wise counsel or even professional counseling. Your procedures should always contain a level of protection for your people. Even adults can be obnoxious online, but teenagers can take it to levels adults are sometimes not even aware. We pray that you can find ways to prevent bullying in ministry. Although we desire for you never to need to report anyone, the law for mandatory reporting is specific and minister or volunteer, it's crucial that you understand the rules. Supervision does not need to become a helicopter parenting model, but we do need to be aware of the surroundings and activity of the environment where your teenagers gather. Policies are not easy but needed when we have recurring aspects that merit our attention. Teenagers can be hard to keep up with, especially when they are clueless or desire to elude your watchful care. Emergencies and unexpected events can occur so developing plans will help you handle the rare occurrence. The culture is always shifting with each generation. The facilities can fail us as we seek to respond to the present reality and needs of youth ministry. Trips are not as easy as "just winging it," and require planning and thoughtful execution to prevent "trip-ups." Negating negligence is a reality, so do your homework to be sure you are not negligent in your ministry as a volunteer or minister. We believe understanding issues in your community and interacting within youth culture will help you impact lives for eternity.

Review the considerations, ask questions, pray and see what you can do to enhance your ministry. If you see issues in many areas, begin to prioritize and address them one at a time.

Below, you will find some trusted ministries and resources are provided for you in specific aspects of risk management. As you protect your people, we believe your ministry will be enhanced. We are ministers, not insurance agents or lawyers. The intent is to minister more effectively to reach people and not scare you out of ministry. Shepherd your people in their character, through their concerns and issues, as a watchman, and through the environment and culture. Shalom!

END NOTES

1. Hammar, Richard. "Defending Youth Ministries from 8 Critical Risks."

2. John W. Ritenbaugh, Psalm 23 (Part 3) in Forerunner Commentary, accessed 2.26.16 at https://www.bibletools.org/index.cfm/fuseaction/Topical.show/RTD/cgg/ID/14587/Shepherds-Staff-Used-fo r-Inspection.htm

3. https://www.washingtonpost.com/opinions/the-gop-is-learning-that-character-matters/2016/06/16/58b7b97c-33e4-11e6-8758-d58e76e11b12_story.html?utm_term=.1c2f91a90802

4. Paul Cedar, "Accountability That Makes Sense" in CT Pastors (online), http://www.christianitytoday.com/pastors/books/mastering pastoral/mstmin04-7.html , accessed 12/28/16. Copyright © 1991 by Christianity Today.

5. An Analysis of Youth Ministers' Perceptions of Character Qualities, Leadership Competencies, and Leadership Flaws that Facilitate or Hinder Effective Youth Ministry, EdD Dissertation, Southern Baptist Theological Seminary, 2007.

6. Thomas Paine (1737-1809) English intellectual. Quote located at http://en.proverbia.net/citastema.asp?tematica=176, accessed 12/28/16.

7. Robert Heiliger, PCC-S, "It's Time to Refer When . . ." From the website of the Professional Pastoral-Counseling Institute, Inc., http://www.pastoral-counseling.org/asp/page.asp?ID=1108, accessed 12/29/16.

8. Ibid

9. Several bullets informed by Richard Hammar, "What Youth Pastors Should Know About Counseling" Church Law and Tax Report, http://www.churchlawandtax.com/lessons/content/what-youth-pastors-should-know-about-counseling.html, accessed 12/29/16.

10. Pollack, William S. Real Boys' Voices (New York, NY: Penguin Books, 2000), 107.

11. www.nea.org/statistics

12. Stopbullying.gov/at-risk/effects/index.html

13. https://www.stopbullying.gov.at-risk.warning-signs/index.html

14. For more information on mandated reporters, see Child Welfare Information Gateway's Mandatory Reporters of Child Abuse and Neglect at https://www.childwelfare.gov/topics/systemwide/laws-policies/statutes/manda/.

15. https://www.childwelfare.gov/pubPDFs/clergymandated.pdf#page=1&view=Introduction

16. Isla Wallace and Lisa Bunting, "An examination of local, national and international arrangements for the mandatory reporting of child abuse: the implications for Northern Ireland" a paper presented to the NSPCC Northern Ireland, August 2007. https://www.nspcc.org.uk/globalassets/documents/research-reports/mandatory-reporting-research-ni.pdf, accessed 12/28/16.

17. http://www.brotherhoodmutual.com/index.cfm/resources/ministry-safety/article/mandated-reporting/

18. https://www.childwelfare.gov/pubs/factsheets/whatiscan/, accessed 10/26/18

19. Ibid.

20. https://www.childwelfare.gov/topics/responding/reporting/how/, accessed 12/29/16

21. Robert H. Welch, Serving by Safeguarding Your Church. (Grand Rapids, Zondervan, 2002), 51.

22. Robert H. Welch, Church Administration, 2nd ed. (Nashville: Broadman and Holman Academic, 2005), 57.

23. Ibid., 58.

24. Conley, Kim. "Top 6 Check-In Software Security Options." Church Tech Today Technology for Today's Church, June 20, 2012. Accessed August 26, 2016. http://www.churchtechtoday.com/2012/06/20/top-6-childrens-checkin-software-security-options/

25. James F. Cobble, Jr. and Richard Hammar, Risk Management Handbook for Churches and Schools, (Carol Stream: IL, Christianity Today, 2007), 362.

26. Ibid., 364.

27. Jack Crabtree Better Safe than Sued (Copyright 2008 by the Livingstone Corporation. Distributed by Youth Specialties Resources, El Cajon, CA).

28. A good discussion of the decision and its impact on churches is on the Church Law and Tax website, http://www.churchlawandtax.com/blog/2015/june/what-churches-and-clergy-should-note-from-same-sex-marriage.html

29. http://www.usatoday.com/story/news/politics/2016/05/12/feds-schools-transgender-bathrooms-letter-title-ix/84311104/

SUGGESTED RESOURCES FOR RISK MANAGEMENT

1. Ministrysafe referenced in the book: http://ministrysafe.com/

2. Church law and tax has numerous legal resources that are helpful: http://www.churchlawandtax.com

3. Guidestone has resources for mission trip coverage as well as many helpful downloads within their safety toolkit: finances: http://www.guidestonepropertycasualty.org/SafetyToolkit

4. Church Mutual has several resources for Risk Control available for download: https://www.churchmutual.com/98/Safety-Resources

5. Brotherhood Mutual Insurance has templates for forms and policy for youth ministry: https://www.brotherhoodmutual.com/index.cfm/resources/ministry-safety/children-youth/

6. Ready.gov has many resources and preparation techniques for various disasters such as weather, active shooters, power outages, and more.

ABOUT THE AUTHORS

Dr. Jody Dean, serves as an Associate Professor for Christian Education at New Orleans Baptist Theological Seminary. Dr. Dean has years of ministry experience including ministry leadership, youth, discipleship, and administration. He is also the Senior Regional Associate Dean for Extension Centers at NOBTS. He is married to Emily and they have two kids Lydia and James Robert.

Dr. Allen Jackson is currently the pastor of Dunwoody Baptist Church in Atlanta, GA. But for many years he shaped and led the youth ministry initiatives of New Orleans Baptist Theological Seminary as a professor and the head of the Youth Ministry Institute. Allen likes golf, computers, running, drinking coffee, and snow skiing.

Allen is the husband of one wife (Judi), the father of two children (Aaron, born in 1988 and Sarah, born in 1991), and as of the publishing of this book, a new grandfather.

AS A YOUTH MINISTER, YOU WANT TO LEAD STUDENTS TO BE MORE LIKE CHRIST.

THE QUESTION IS, HOW DO YOU GO ABOUT DOING IT?

DISCIPLE: The Ordinary Person's Guide to Discipling Teenagers is a practical, down-to-earth guide for leading teenagers to pursue Christ.

GET SERIOUS ABOUT DISCIPLE-MAKING IN YOUR MINISTRY WITH *DISCIPLE*.

FOR SAMPLES & ORDERING INFO, GO TO YM360.COM/DISCIPLE.

YOUTH MINISTRY IS NOT FOR THE FAINT OF HEART.

WHICH IS WHY *CONSIDER THIS* IS SUCH AN IMPORTANT BOOK.

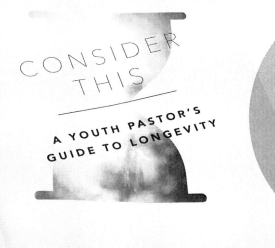

CONSIDER THIS is an essential resource for anyone starting out in youth ministry, and a great guide for anyone looking to mentor another youth worker.

CONSIDER THIS IS PACKED WITH PRACTICAL, INSIGHTFUL WISDOM ON HOW TO EXCEL AT BEING A YOUTH MINISTER, SUCH AS:

- Establishing and maintaining boundaries
- Establishing a great relationship with your pastor
- Getting and staying organized
- Recruiting Leaders and Volunteers
- And much, much more

YM360.COM *OR* CALL 888.969.6360

GENERATE
CAMP BY YM360

5 DAYS OF CAMP THAT CAN CHANGE THE OTHER 51 WEEKS OF YOUR YEAR, YOUR LIFE, AND MAYBE EVEN YOUR GENERATION.

GENERATESTUDENTS.COM